TALES FROM THE HEART

Pet Relationship Love Stories

SUZANNE THIBAULT

Four Paws Publishing

Tales from the Heart–Pet Relationship Love Stories

Copyright © 2022 by Suzanne Thibault

All Rights Reserved

No part of this book may be reproduced or transmitted in any form or by any means, electronic or mechanical, including photocopying or recording, without written permission from the author.

For more information about this book or the author, visit:

www.suzannethibault.net

Four Paws Publishing

www.fourpawspublishing.net

(P) ISBN 978-1-7341721-2-6

(E) ISBN 978-1-7341721-3-3

Printed in the United States of America, First Printing 2021

Cover Design: Tramaine Lott

Cover Photo: Pexels.com

Editing: Marsha Fulton, Mypurplepen Editing

Disclaimer: Information in this book is intended for informational purposes only. The views and opinions expressed in this book are those of the author and guest authors. Any content provided by the authors is of their opinion and is not intended to malign any religion, ethnic group, club, organization, company, individual, or anyone or anything. The author will not be held liable for any advice, suggestions, wisdom, opinions, or omissions in this book.

ACKNOWLEDGMENTS

There is community in many voices coming together in a united way. It has been my honor and privilege to work with these amazing Guest Chapter Authors and their pets who shared their personal relationship stories. I wish to thank these incredible authors for sharing their inspiring stories of love. Thank you for entrusting me to bring forth and share your tales from the heart. I am grateful to God for the many blessings in bringing together the right people and their pets for this project that illustrate inspirational relationship stories of love.

I want to thank my husband and daughter for all their encouragement and loving support. Thank you to Odie, Abby, Lily, Jack, and Luna, the Fab Five, for your furry support and guidance. I thank God for the foundation of love upon which I stand. It is His grace that has touched the pages of the book, bringing love to life.

FOREWORD

Any pet lover will tell you their pet is a member of their family. We have considered pets to be human beings' best friends and family members for a long time. We have fun with our pets, laugh, cry and cuddle with them. Living daily life with furry family members brings joy to our lives.

Animal lovers understand the sanctuary of love your pet provides. As pet relationships grow, you realize how similar your lives are. You both have unique personalities, feelings, and emotions. The relationship you share with your pet is something you realize radically changes your life.

In the eyes of an animal, you can see your own vulnerability and find yourself. Animals teach you how to be a better friend and have healthy personal relationships. You see the beauty and wonder in life, just like your cat, who gazes at dust sparkles floating in the air. Your pet has instant forgiveness of all your faults, teaching you to offer that same forgiveness to others. You realize your pet is teaching you about life.

Animals help you understand you are a part of this world, sharing a heart and soul connection with all of life. Animals explain the mysteries of life for us, teaching us how to live a more heart-centered, caring, and giving life. In caring for animals, you learn to care for yourself and others. The loving relationship you share with your pet is a catalyst of personal and spiritual growth for you and your family.

1

THE PURPOSE OF PETS

I have always believed that pets have a purpose even more important than what we might understand. It is easy to see pets as our companions. They love following you around the house, cuddling next to you on the couch, and enjoy living life with you. Pets are more than our companions though; they prefer to be seen as our partners in this journey called life.

Part of a pet's purpose is obvious. They provide many forms of comfort and nurturing. Pets have a natural talent in providing health benefits to us humans:

Pets provide comfort. Animals provide comfort to us by simply being with us in a non-judgmental state. They know that simply lying next to you brings you great comfort. Petting your pet helps take your mind off worries and refocus on what's important. When you feel sad, your pet is right beside you, comforting you with their warm presence.

Pets encourage nurturing. The simple act of taking care of a pet develops nurturing and compassion. You want what's best for your pet and care about their happiness. That makes it easy to develop deeper compassion. When you care for your pet, it allows you to open your heart to care more for others.

Pets are family. Animals provide you with social interaction when other people are not around. Your pet's companionship helps you to see that you are never alone. They love hanging out with you and being your best friend. Pets love partnering with you in life as a member of your family.

Pets provide stress relief. Pets help you reduce stress by refocusing your attention on them. This helps you let go of stress and relax simply by petting them. The physical act of petting your pet is soothing, as it helps you relax, slow your breathing, and calm your mind.

Pets encourage exercise. A Michigan State University study found one benefit of having a pet is that people who own dogs exercise about half an hour more per week. That is certainly true in our family. With two dogs, we are walking every day, which benefits them and us. Pets help us lead an active lifestyle.

One of the biggest benefits pets provide to us is often unexpected. It is the personal relationship you share with your pet based on the firm foundation of unconditional love.

Psychology refers to unconditional love as a state of mind in which you have the goal of increasing the welfare of another, despite any benefit to yourself. You can see and experience your pet's unconditional love each day. They give love freely, no matter what state of mind you are in. Your pet might frustrate you, but they will always make the first move to be near you to comfort you. How beautiful it must be to be a pet and share love so freely! Animals are excellent role models on how to live life.

Pets can help a family become closer to each other. A pet is often the center of activity for the family. Everyone can walk the dog together, share in the care of their pet's feeding and grooming, or play with the pet. Family life can be hectic. Spending time with your pet offers the potential to help you slow down and enjoy life more.

The personal connection you share with your pet is spiritually profound. We base pet relationships on love, a heart-to-heart connection. I asked my dog, Abby, a Rat Terrier mix, what she believes a pet's spiritual purpose is:

"Animals help you tap into a part of your heart that you might not reach yourself. That part of you is the divine love you hold inside to share with others. Pet relationships stand upon unconditional love, which helps you see the truth of who you really are. The real purpose of pets is to surround you with love, to help you express more love." -Abby

Abby is talking about the personal, spiritual relationship we share with animals. Pets can have many purposes and gifts they provide to us as our family members. Knowing that when I hang out with Abby, she's helping me connect to a part of myself at a deeper level is a genuine gift. Now I know that the true purpose of pets is simply to help us love more. Ultimately, pets help us express more love, and that is a generous purpose for pets.

2
ANIMALS ARE MESSENGERS OF SPIRIT

Animals are God's creation. Our job is to love, honor, and appreciate them as sentient souls we share life with. Our pets carry Spirit's love and wisdom that they express to us. We are all a part of God's love, and Spirit partners with pets to help us be better people. Animals express unconditional love, which is a gift of Spirit. Animals are amazing in their ability to love, a visual, cuddly example of love we can learn from.

Understanding that animals are messengers of Spirit can have a profound impact when you realize Spirit speaks through animals. We can more easily receive loving messages from Spirit through our pets. I learned this from my personal experience as a child.

At age eight, my toxic parents took a trip to Tahiti, leaving me home alone to fend for myself. This caused deep abandonment trauma. I screamed in fear, and my childhood dog Wiggles softly said to me, "Do not be afraid. You are not alone. I am here with you, and I love you." I gazed into Wiggles' eyes and felt her love. Me hearing those words helped me to survive the trauma.

As a child, I did not know God. If I had heard a strange voice saying those words, it would have scared me. With Wiggles right there with me, I looked into her eyes and knew it was Wiggles speaking to me. I knew she loved me, so hearing those loving words was natural. This helped me receive the message and feel better. That was Spirit's grace overflowing with love. As an adult, I realize that was both Spirit and Wiggles together saying those words to me, and my heart bursts with love and gratitude. The Holy Spirit's grace flows through our pets for our benefit.

Grace, which is Holy Spirit's love and kindness, provides strength through the power of love to overcome adversity. Animals help provide Holy Spirit's unconditional love to us, including His grace and mercy. The world would be a darker place without animals by our side. Animals help us be less afraid in our relationship with Spirit.

Pets display many spiritual qualities through their behavior. They let you know you are never alone, that you are very loved no matter what, that you are forgiven when you do wrong. God sends animal messengers as representatives of these virtues which actually are His. If you are stressed out, overwhelmed or upset, remember that Spirit sends these furry, feathery, scaley faces with a generous heart to support you. Your pet is an ambassador of Spirit's love and wisdom that brings you closer to Spirit.

It seems such a brilliant gift that our Creator has provided four legged family members to support us in life. Our pets are our angels in disguise, four legged therapists, and cuddle commanders who help ease our burdens in life. We just look into their beautiful eyes and smile, knowing we are loved. Now take that love from your pet and realize that Holy Spirit is there too, loving you unconditionally. Inside your pet's eyes is also Spirit's eyes loving gazing upon you. All this so you can realize you are loved!

Your pet is a role model of Spirit's love, teaching you about love. Pet love is sincere, never ending, always present, attentive, caring, and comforting. In this way your pet is acting as your soul's guardian angel, protecting what is most important, your heart and soul. Your pet is making sure you understand, embrace and share more love!

What beautiful gifts pets are in our lives. Once you have lived with and loved a pet, your life will never be the same. If you allow yourself to see Holy Spirit's love inside your pet, you open the door to His love.

3
ALL ANIMALS FEEL EMOTIONS

Animals are sentient, meaning they can feel and experience emotions. Gandhi once said, "The greatness of a nation and its moral progress can be judged by the way its animals are treated." Those of us who love and appreciate animals understand those words. Scientists have long realized that emotional experiences, such as pleasure and pain, are not unique to human beings. Animals also can understand and experience fear, sadness, anxiety, excitement, and joy, a full range of emotions.

What you see in your pet's behavior tells you a lot about what is happening inside your pet's mind and heart. You usually know how your pet feels because we recognize animals feel emotions. If you are empathic, then you can feel how your pet feels.

The scientific study of animal intelligence, emotions, and social behavior has made gigantic leaps forward over the years. In 2012, a prominent group of scientists got together and signed The Cambridge Declaration on Consciousness. This declaration recognized that animals are conscious beings with feelings and emotions. The evidence to support this is overwhelming.

If you live with a pet, I am sure you have witnessed that life can be very intense for animals. They have deep emotions and feelings. Animals can stand up for themselves when challenged. They love unconditionally. They get excited when you return home and feel sadness when losing a loved one. Your pet's presence in your life is hugely rewarding and enriching. The love you share with your pet is profound through the feelings you share.

It has been many years since the Declaration on Consciousness. What has changed for animals? Societal change has been slow. The World Animal Protection group has created an interactive world map (https://api.worldanimalprotection.org/) showing the progress of legal protections for animals worldwide. The map ranks countries based upon animal protection laws and animal welfare standards. I am dismayed to say that the United States ranks incredibly low, with only a few states enacting animal welfare laws. Other countries are doing much better.

When I think of the millions of food industry animals or animals used in product testing, it hurts my heart knowing they are all feeling pain and suffering at the hands of humans. The Humane Society states that cosmetic tests on animals are banned globally in 37 countries, which is good news. They estimate that hundreds of thousands of small animals are cruelly tested upon around the world each year. When I think about how those animals must feel, it breaks my heart.

Millions upon millions of animals each year are treated like objects, seen only as a commodity. If people could see the animal's emotional pain, our world would be a much different place because we would have more human compassion in the world. It can be a hard, slow process to bring positive change to the world. I believe minor changes can make a difference. The easiest way to bring change is to be the change yourself.

One way I bring change as an animal advocate is through my own choices. I advocate for animals by eating a vegan diet. As a child, I grew up in a meat-eating home. I have been eating vegan for about 14 years. Upon switching to a plant-based diet, I lost 35 pounds and have not been sick in all those years. That is a win for my physical body and a win from my compassionate heart for all animals.

Eating vegan is right for me, although it is not right for everyone. Today, almost every restaurant offers a vegetarian or vegan meal option. Grocery stores sell accidentally vegan snacks and various vegan protein options. It is easy to be vegan now, and I highly recommend it. I do not judge anyone who eats differently, as my own family is omnivore. I believe everyone should eat in a way that is healthiest for them. For me, being vegan means, I support animals because I feel that no animals' life is less important than my own. My compassion for all living beings leads me to be vegan. The positive health benefits are outstanding.

Animals are not here to experiment on or abuse. I love and adore animals and advocate for their welfare. I also have made a choice to stop buying products from companies that perform animal testing. There are many companies that are cruelty-free, many huge brand names you know and probably enjoy. I switched brands I use and now feel much better supporting animals through supporting cruelty-free brands. You, too, can help animals through the choice of the products you use.

The places you can research cruelty-free products include crueltyfreekitty.com, crueltyfreeinternational.org, and crueltyfree.peta.org. Cruelty-Free International is working to end animal experiments worldwide. PETA's website is excellent as they have PDF lists that you can download of companies that test on animals. They also have a free vegan starter kit with recipes. Cruelty-free Kitty has a good blog and a list of approved cruelty-free brands through their criteria.

While there is still room for improvement worldwide for protecting animal rights, we can all do our part to support animals through the product and food choices we make, taking steps in the right direction for a more humane, compassionate society. By making smarter choices, you help prevent injustice against animals.

It takes everyone in a community to care. Think about how you can support animals in a bigger way. When you visit places with captive animals such as the zoo, circus, shelter, pet store, amusement park, farm, or anywhere animals are in the wild, think about how they feel and what their life experiences might be like. Look into the eyes of those animals and let your compassion and respect lead your personal choices. Let animals everywhere know that you honor, respect, cherish, and love them. Your simple choices can make a world of difference and deepen your relationship with all of life.

4
OUR EMPATHIC CONNECTION

Empathy is a multifaceted feeling of emotions. We human beings live in a world submerged in a constant media stream of television and movie violence, destruction, and despair. This can cause steady desensitization to other people's suffering. It is often easier to feel empathy for suffering animals than people.

Do you get angry hearing animal abuse stories? We naturally draw our empathy to the innocent and those we perceive as helpless and vulnerable. Our hearts go out to animals in need, and we want to help. As human beings, we feel compelled to protect children and animals. It is our innate human desire to protect and nurture those who are innocent and vulnerable.

Beyond our desire to care for animals, what else is going on? Unconditional love. Who is always happy to see you? Who never judges you? Who makes you laugh when you are feeling down? Who cuddles next to you when feeling sick? Who has no expectations of you other than to love you? Your pet.

It's hard to give and receive unconditional love in human relationships because of the mental baggage we carry, such as judgment, assumptions, and expectations. Animal relationships make unconditional love easy. They allow us to be who we are without judgment.

> **Animals help us tap into a part of our heart
> we might not be able to reach ourselves.**

Animals help us connect to the most intimate area of our hearts, that place of empathic love, nurturing, and caring, a place we sometimes keep hidden to feel safe. They help us grow our compassion, inspiring us to reveal deeper love to others. Animals make it easy for us to love them and learn unconditional love by helping us to open our hearts.

Empathy is a superpower for both you and your pet. Because you share feelings, you can focus upon your empathic abilities to understand how your pet is feeling. Empathy is a part of your intuitive nature, your inner wisdom. You feel things naturally, understand feelings and how other people feel. You can do this with your pet too, on a more subtle level.

Human beings have a deep capacity to love that we tend to forget about. We must learn to lead from love, tap into it and express it with intention. Our pet relationships support us in being more loving. Empathic feelings are always turned on, meaning you are always feeling. It is this way for everyone. Some people ignore their feelings as it can feel overwhelming. Love feels good, so let's all share more love.

If you are an empath who has issues with feeling too much, know that is common. Empaths can sense both the visible and the invisible, always tuned into feelings. It is the same thing for your pet. All this unconscious sharing of feelings is amazing. When you understand the depth of empathic sharing, you can understand just how much your pet supports you. That empathic connection is unbreakable, so it is important to learn to understand it.

Animals communicate through feelings. Feelings are emotions in motion. Emotions carry a frequency wavelength from the heart. The HeartMath® Institute has scientifically proven this. The heart is the source of both human and animal empathic abilities, how you are connected with your pet.

Notice this empathic connection you share with your pet. That connection is a language of feelings. Just as human beings have subtle feelings, so do animals. When you tune into those subtle feelings of your pet, it empowers you. This is especially helpful when your pet is sick or misbehaving. This can provide you better understanding of the situation.

Feelings are a natural part of being human. May you embrace your empathic pet connection and allow it to deepen your relationship. You share a magical relationship with your pet that broadens your awareness and perspective. That is a genuine gift of support from your empathic pet.

5
PETS AS LIFE PARTNERS

The most magical aspect of your pet relationship is the awareness you develop about your pet and yourself, which changes your life for the better. Your awareness of understanding your empathic pet's behavior changes your perspective. Who knew the pets we share life with are supporting us so much.

Pets provide us with both psychological and physical benefits. Some cats live in nursing homes that support seniors who have given up. There are animals who work in airports to calm fear of flying; pets who visit hospitals or courtrooms to bring comfort; children can practice reading to pets; guide dogs and cats who support their people with their motor skills, physical balance, attention, alerts, and overall health. These public displays of support by pets are beautiful. They show us exactly how our pets support our personal lives!

When you adopt a pet, they are excited and happy to become a part of your family. Your pet sees you as a family member whom they love. Because animals lead their lives from a place of unconditional love, they view their human family with compassion and empathy. Your pet understands when you feel down or unhappy and will try to cheer you up. When I feel down, my dog Abby will jump in my lap and act goofy, making me laugh. Laughter always makes me feel better!

In understanding that animals are empathic, your perspective about your relationship changes. I am sure if you have a dog or cat, they do things that make you laugh, but maybe you never saw this behavior as trying to support you to feel happier. You just see this as your pet's goofy behavior. Now, look at the bigger picture. Your pet is supporting you as a life partner, sharing life with you, helping you shift your perspective and mood.

You can expand your awareness of your pet's role in your life. The next time your pet makes you laugh, think about how you felt the moment before. Did you have a rough day that left you feeling stressed out? Your pet just might be working to uplift how you feel by making you laugh! As our partners in life, pets have a mission to provide emotional support to their human family members. Your recognition of this deepens your relationship with your pet.

An animal's behavior is communication.

You can learn to see and understand your pet's support as loving guidance. Our pets are helping us to learn and grow on a spiritual level. Here are some ways you can interpret your pet's guidance that is speaking to you:

- When your pet stalls from coming inside when called, they might be teaching patience.
- If your dog's excessive barking frustrates you, they might be teaching tolerance.
- When your pet makes you laugh, they are helping you laugh and lift your mood.
- If your cat lays down on your laptop keyboard, they might be asking you to take a needed break.
- If your cat knocks a book off the bookshelf, they might be suggesting a book to read.

- If your pet attempts to grab your attention, they might be helping you redirect your thoughts.

You know and understand your pet's daily behaviors. Now take a deeper look at those behaviors to see how much your pet is supporting you. This is a behavioral form of communication that your pet is using to speak to you. Your pet is not judging you. Animals just want us to be happy. It takes awareness to notice this form of communication and a willingness to look inside yourself. Will you allow your pet to be your life partner who supports you in becoming a better person? Your life partnership with your pet can transform your life. Your pet's love, guidance, and support are beautiful gifts! Pets bring out the best in us.

6
PET RELATIONSHIP LOVE STORIES

For the past decade, I have had the pleasure of supporting many animal lovers and their pets. It always amazes me how having a conversation with your pet is healing. There are so many beautiful, heartwarming pet relationship stories I have encountered. Some have made me cry, some have made me laugh, many have left me in wonder at the depth of love a person and their pet share.

The following chapters are written by Guest Chapter Authors who share their unique pet relationship love stories with their pet's perspective. They are stories of loss, reunion, partnership, heartbreak, and joy. The overarching theme of all these relationships is love, a love so deep it is personally transformative. The authors realize how much their pet supports and teaches them about life. They understand their pet's perspective empowers them in the care of their pet. Most of all, these animal lovers understand how a pet's love helps their heart to heal, grow, and express more love.

May you find inspiration in these stories to help you better understand your animal relationships. You will discover that relationships happen not only with our pets but with wild animals too!

7
ANDY THE SUPPORTIVE LIFE PARTNER
BY JOY HOWARD AND ANDY

Andy

Andy was a female black Labrador whom we adored. She was a big fur shedder, spreading her fur everywhere. As a gentle dog, she was kind to everyone. At age twelve, she developed coordination problems, so I called Suzanne to speak with Andy about her health. Andy told me she was ready to cross the rainbow bridge and was asking for help.

I called a home visit vet who performed euthanasia so Andy would be more comfortable passing at home. We laid a sheet down on the floor for Andy to lay upon. What was interesting was we had a Cockatiel bird named Albert. Before the vet arrived, Albert was flying around and around Andy, and one of Albert's feathers fell out and fell, right on top of her. I think Albert was saying goodbye to Andy.

When the vet arrived, he shaved Andy's leg and inserted the IV, which blew the vein, causing pain for Andy, who began whining. I thought this would be a peaceful process for Andy, and my heart ached at her suffering. Andy, the Lab, crossed over the rainbow bridge. Heavy grief filled my heart in losing her. She was gone.

Suzanne was driving down the freeway when Andy's spirit zoomed into her intuition with a message for me. Suzanne called me while driving to explain that Andy's soul said, *"Tell them I'm coming back!"* It was such amazing news that helped me to feel better.

About one week later, Andy told Suzanne that she was coming back around November 23. So as time got closer, it thrilled us she was going to come back to us. I had always dreamed of having a Miniature Schnauzer because they do not shed. I had read somewhere that wire-haired dogs do not shed, so I wanted a non-shedding dog because Andy, the Lab, had shed so much, and it was so much work. I didn't mind cleaning up because I loved her, but if I had a choice, I would like a dog that did not do that.

As November 23rd approached, we learned that Andy in spirit said to check our County Animal Shelter that day, and there would be a scruffy, dirty little dog. So now we knew where to look. It amazed me that Andy was so precise with information on how we could find her.

Scruffy was okay with me because I like scruffy dogs. Suzanne met us at the shelter on November 23. We were so excited! We went inside and began looking at the dogs. There was a beautiful Otter Hound who looked scruffy. Suzanne asked me what I felt with that dog, and I felt nothing, so we moved on. Finally, we came upon a stall with five small dogs inside. One dog was scruffy and very dirty-looking, having just arrived at the shelter that morning. We took that dog into the shelter's family room for a meet and greet. This dog had beige fur with obvious dirt, having just come off the streets. He was skinny, about 10 pounds. I sat down and called out, "Andy?" The dog ran and jumped into my arms! It was the most exciting leap of joy I have ever seen! It was so magical and truly a confirmation of unending love.

Andy, the Wire-Haired Terrier, says, *"That day truly was magical! The moment I laid eyes upon Joy from behind bars, I knew we had been divinely reunited. We both could sense the loving soul-to-soul connection we share. I had heard Joy saying she wanted a non-shedding dog, and here I appeared, dirty and scruffy just for her!"*

While Andy the Terrier had a lot of similar mannerisms as Andy the Lab, he also came with his share of new life experiences that shaped his behavior. To this day, Andy will not go into a bathroom. Andy replied, *"Yes, this is true. Current life experiences influence how you live your life. That is the same for people and animals. Life experiences influence behavior."*

Andy is the most intuitive dog. He is good at showing it. I will say, "You want to come with me today," and he gets excited, or "You have to stay home," and he will sit down. He understands what I am saying. I tell him, "You're the man of the house here; take care of things," and he's like, "I know." Andy understands we are companions because he always wants to snuggle. He's always there with me, and I never feel alone.

Andy the Terrier says, *"I most appreciate this lifetime with Joy because it's so filled with love, and the two of us share the deepest love. This is something I love; we understand each other, appreciate each other, and love each other. I see myself as more than a companion to Joy. I see us as life partners."*

I think Andy and I are together because we have a soul contract. I believe Andy the Lab saw our sorrow when she was transitioning over the rainbow bridge because we had a profound connection with her. I believe Andy the Terrier wants to continue our relationship as a healer and to keep my energy up.

Andy replied, *"You nailed it on the head, Mom. The Holy Spirit showed me. I did not want to leave Joy alone through life's struggles. I wanted to be there with her, supporting her through life's challenges, because I knew my love could help carry Joy through it. I came back to be with Joy and be an emotional support system for her."*

Andy does such a good job at that! He's such the perfect dog. He is my travel partner. He gets along with other dogs and cats. Andy is a happy, healthy dog who loves life. Plus, he does not shed!

A few years ago, Andy taught me something important. I was nervous about living in a rental home, so I did not unpack my things. I thought I might move again soon. My husband was very sick. I did not feel comfortable renting a home, as it did not feel like mine. I had not unpacked for months. Andy was potty trained, but he began peeing on the wall right in front of me and stare right at me while he did it. This upset me very much. It turns out Andy was telling me to take ownership of the home. I did not understand what that meant at first. I later realized taking ownership meant it was time for me to unpack and decorate the home as my own! I began unpacking and decorating the home with my items. Andy never peed again! Andy taught me to make my house a home so that I could feel comfortable there. This story shows us that pets guide us. We may not understand their message right away. Once we understand the message, we can move forward, and then our pet stops giving us the message. Both our lives changed for the better.

Andy says, *"That is my favorite story, too! It shows the power of the animal-human relationship. When you hear your pet's perspective, it helps brings change to your own life. Understanding your pet's wisdom changes both of your lives."*

After I decorated and cleaned up the rental home, I noticed that my creativity returned, and positive change started happening. Pet guidance is one of the most significant learning experiences of my relationship with Andy.

Andy and I have a big relationship of love. He guides me, and we have an intelligent relationship. Love is what I need most in my life, and I appreciate Andy being here with me.

Andy gushed love to Joy and said, "*My relationship with Joy is the most endearing love of all, the greatest love of all, the most heartwarming love of all. No greater love is shared, except with Spirit. The human/animal relationship of love is unconditional. It teaches every human being to love others unconditionally. I appreciate the love that I share with Joy. We can gaze into each other's eyes and understand each other, know what each other needs. I know what she needs if she's feeling stressed out. Joy knows what I need when she sees me behaving in certain ways. This unspoken, empathic relationship is beautiful, strong, and powerful. It is a life partnership for both of us. I love you, Joy!*"

Andy is my best friend. He is a beautiful, wise soul who understands love and teaches me so much. The love that we share is amazing. We are life partners!

8
THE SHENANIGANS OF SNAP AND CRACKLE

BY CHERYL MEYER AND JOHN GINS, SNAP, AND CRACKLE

Snap and Crackle

I, Cheryl, got autoimmune disease many years ago, so I did a lot of research on toxins. I realized I wanted to share my research with others, which inspired me to become a Certified Integrative Health and Wellness Coach. My research led me to write two multiple award-winning books: *It Feels Good to Feel Good: Learn to Eliminate Toxins, Reduce Inflammation and Feel Great Again,* and *Feeling Good: Living Low Toxin in Community and Everyday Life.*

My research showed me that toxins also affected the three kitties that I had. All three of them died early at ages 12, 14, and 16. I have had cats my whole life, many of whom made it into their 20s. My friends used to joke that they wanted to come back in their next life as my cat. Unfortunately, two cats died of cancer, and Beeper, who lived to 16, had kidney disease and possibly cancer. I researched toxins for our fur babies for my second book since I knew that all the toxins must have harmed my kitties in their lives, and I wanted to give any future kitties a healthier, longer life.

I had married John three years before my three cats passed. After Beeper died, John told me he was deathly allergic to cats, so I thought I would never have another cat. John was on medications for his allergies. John replied, "My allergies were so bad I could be within one mile of Cheryl's house, and my allergies would act up. I got tested for my sensitivities. On a scale of 1 to 25, I was over one hundred for cats, so I knew I was very allergic to them."

John continued, "After reading Suzanne's book, *Animal Wisdom Tales: Messages of Love from Pets and Wild Animals*, I began thinking about pet relationships and how connected Cheryl was to her three previous cats. Right before COVID began, I started researching to see if I could find a non-allergic cat breed. There were about seven breeds on the list that were low allergy. Oriental Short Hair cats are on the list, so I checked on Pet Finder. I put in a request to locate that breed of cat. Less than two months later, up pops an answer for a cat that is 25 miles away! He was a male Ginger Oriental Short Hair kitten. I immediately sent Cheryl a message about this kitten. I was so excited! Cheryl agreed we should meet the kitten. Cheryl then discovered this kitten had a brother, so she asked if they could adopt them both. The foster home was thrilled! Snap and Crackle are inseparable brothers and play with each other constantly. They were about eight weeks old when we adopted them."

I talked to Suzanne, who told me Snap was a young soul and Crackle was an old soul, which is so true. Crackle is very calm. He likes to come and sit on me but is not demanding or anything. He wants to be close. Snap will climb all over me. He flies onto me, sometimes without warning, and I am never quite ready for it. Both Snap and Crackle are adorable and very sweet. They are almost identical. Snap has slightly whiter paws. Crackle has slightly bigger ears. In personality, they are different. Snap and Crackle laugh. Snap says,

"I love, love, love that story. It is so magical the way Mom and Dad found us. It was meant to be. We are destined to be together." Crackle adds, "You both immediately noticed how different our personalities are, kind of like the both of you. We compliment you and your family. As a part of your family, we are all loving each other, and we get along great."

Snap and Crackle are both connected at the hip. They will lie on the bed for their afternoon nap with Snap cleaning Crackle's ears for an hour. Crackle says, "We are best friends on a soul level. We both wanted to come into life together and experience life as an adventure. We landed in Cheryl and John's family, which feels divinely arranged."

John shares, "Well, I have never had an allergic reaction to the cats, and that to me is a miracle. I do not need medication. I ended up buying some allergy meds just in case, and I have not even opened the bottle. I only have an allergic reaction to Snap and Crackle when I am scratched, which is amazing."

It is truly astounding how we found these cats, and John's allergies are fine. It means we are supposed to be together as a family. The cats bring us great joy. In the morning, Snap usually hangs out with me, and Crackle hangs with John. We both have our respective cats for a while, which is extremely cute. If John comes into my office to talk with me, Snap is immediately on me to protect me.

"I am not protecting you. I am showing John that I am your main man," Snap laughs, "even though I know you prefer human men! I am a bundle of joy, an adventurous soul. I love to explore and have adventures, which is why I am so active. Cheryl always laughs at my crazy behaviors, so it is a good thing." Crackle adds, "Our activity also expresses the importance of exercising and being active. I am happy that my human parents are both staying active."

Crackle continues, "It was divinely ordered on a soul level that we were to be together. It was not by chance that you found us on Pet Finder. It was magical! Snap and I are your soul family. We are here to bring joy to our family. Fun is a reminder that you can play and laugh all the time in life, not just sometimes, but every day. It is our goal in life within our family to have fun and adventures."

We have a second home in Sedona, Arizona. Our cats ride with us on the seven-hour drive from Los Angeles, California. They are so good, never saying a peep the entire trip. We talk with Snap and Crackle about traveling a few days in advance so that they know the journey is coming. We place a long tube that goes across the back seat of our vehicle for the cats. They go in with their litter box; they have their food and water, and then relax and sleep the entire way to Arizona and back. Snap says, *"We love traveling to Arizona. It is always a relaxing ride. It is fun to have two homes to explore. We appreciate you telling us before the trips."*

The cats have a cat friend in Arizona named Apollo. He is an outdoor neighbor cat, and he is as big as both of our kitties combined. He will come into our backyard, and both Snap and Crackle get so excited. Apollo's dad feeds Snap and Crackle when we go away overnight.

Snap and Crackle bring us such joy! When I lost my three cats at such young ages, it broke my heart. To have Snap and Crackle now in our life is wonderful. I believe it helped my heart to heal. They have little behaviors that remind me of my previous three cats. Snap replied, *"That is the beauty of pets. We help you heal your heart. Our love helps your heart to heal."*

John says, "Crackle will sit on the back of my chair and tap me on the shoulder with his paw. I stop whatever I am doing, and I will talk to him and pet him. Crackle does not like to get on my lap, but he loves my attention. I see that tap on the shoulder as Crackle making a connection that I appreciate. Then Snap will join in, and the purring begins, giving me so much love. That tap on the shoulder grabs my attention, especially if I have been intensely busy. It tells me I need to stop and take a break. Then both cats trade places, and Snap joins me, and Crackle joins Cheryl. They enjoy giving and receiving love from both of us."

I feel like Snap is teaching me patience because he likes to get into everything. If I am concentrating on work and he interrupts me, it can be a little bit annoying. But Snap is my little sweetheart, so he gets away with murder. Snap replied, *"Yes, you are right, Mom. Patience is good to cultivate."*

Snap also loves to jump. He will jump up on everything from the top of the closet door to the rim of our blinds to the top of the shower door. Crackle has learned to open cabinet doors and drawers to explore. He gets excited when my makeup drawer is open and loves to run off with my makeup sponges. I find them all over the house. They are inexpensive toys that bring him so much joy. Sometimes Snap gets into the act and runs off with Crackle's sponge, but they share well and play well together. We laugh as they are equal opportunity cats.

John says, "During my spiritual studies, I got a reference from somebody saying that both cats and dogs are put on this Earth to be our guides." Snap says, *"It is wonderful that you recognize pets are helping to guide you and see things in your life. I wish more human beings would see how much their pet is supporting their life."*

Crackle and Snap then both explained what is most important about their family relationship. *"Our relationship is made in heaven. It is made of the most important ingredient, unconditional love. The love we all share is powerful, and you can see how much joy it creates. Our relationship is that love lasts throughout all decades. Our love is strong, and it will endure forever. It will never die, it will never leave, it will never end, even though when pets pass, it might seem like it ends. Love truly endures forever. All the wonderful memories we create with each other stay with us. Our love is beautiful, bright love that radiates out into the world. Mom and Dad know that our loving family is helping this world to embrace more love!"*

❧ 9 ❦
MARGOT'S LESSONS OF LOVE
BY MARIE AND MARGOT

Margot

Margot came to live with me because her mom and dad put her outside to live on her own. Her family had grown to include children, and there was no longer room for

Margot. Margot had only known life as an indoor cat and did not know how to be an outdoor cat. It terrified her. The feral cats, who were accustomed to living outdoors, attacked her. They did not like Margot intruding on their territory. Margot was unwanted.

My daughter Kris cares about animals, so Margot's situation was upsetting. One day, knowing that I needed a new friend, Kris went to get Margot. She found her barely surviving outdoors. Kris picked up Margot and brought her home to me.

Margot was scared and such a skinny little kitty. But she was still so beautiful. I felt sorry for Margot and immediately loved her. At the beginning of our relationship, Margot did not trust me or anyone. I did not know if Margot could ever relax. Margot was so frightened. I kept asking Margot to sit with me and let me show her love. Today she will sometimes come and sit by me as I watch TV. By doing that, Margot shows she trusts me.

Margot says, *"Thank you, Marie, for taking me into your family. I am grateful to be with my Mom Marie and her daughters too because they rescued me. I learned a lot from human beings in my earlier life who did not see me as a soul with feelings and emotions. They thought I was a cat, an object. I was not even worth a second thought to them, and my life became very lonely. My situation upset Cathe and Kris. They have big hearts and care about the well-being of animals. Kris said, "Enough is enough," and she was right because I had enough! I felt abandoned in that backyard, uncared for and unloved. I got to come into Marie's home, and I was so grateful. I was also very terrified because of everything I had been through. Marie's love was so gentle. I thank you, Mom, for your enormous love because I knew then that I was in the right place to be a part of your family."*

Margot is intelligent, tender, and loving. She feels my emotions. She is a sweet and smart cat. I've gotten good at seeing the signs Margot uses to communicate. For example, Margot will stand up on her back feet with her front paws in the air. That means she is hungry.

One day Margot ran out the open front door. I live on a busy main street and was anxious that Margot would be injured. I went to the door and called her name. Margot replies, "When I heard Marie call my name, my heart leaped with joy! I realized she wanted me. I turned around and walked into the house, for the first time feeling loved and showing my Mom that I wanted to be there."

I believe animals and humans are supposed to be together. Margot has taught me that some things happen for a reason. No matter the situation, we are together. In this lifetime, things happen a certain way, and I do not know why they happen. Sometimes they are lovely. In this case, it is wonderful living with Margot. Margot and I are together because she knew I could help her. And she realized how much I needed her too. I am so happy we are a family.

Margot replied, "I am with my Mom Marie because she has a caring heart. My mom is correct in saying I needed her. I was so lost and alone. I was praying to find a loving family that would give me love and care. Then, there I was in Marie's house. Someone who would love me rescued me. Mom, you had patience with me and taught me there is another way to live with human beings, and that way is with love. That is what I wanted my whole life. I did not want to live alone in a backyard. I wanted to be with someone who would love me. Marie and I are together because she could help me. It is Marie's caring love that makes us a family."

At night I usually watch TV, and somehow Margot always knows when it is 8 p.m. She tells me it is time to go to bed. Margot gets up and walks into the bedroom. If I don't go there immediately, Margot comes back for me.

Margot is teaching me to have more understanding about life. Margot says, "Yes, I'm teaching my mom to have more patience. Because I am an active cat, it teaches her patience. I also am learning from Marie. She has taught me how to enjoy the little things in life. Earlier in my life, I was in survival mode and could not see the beautiful little things in life. Today I can recognize the simplest things are beautiful. I notice sunlight coming into the room. I see how beautiful it is because it sparkles with particles in the air. I am grateful for how peaceful our life is together. It is those little things that are so important in life that I did not have before. These are gifts I receive and appreciate now because of our relationship of love. Marie and I are sharing this life because we can take care of each other."

Margot continues, *"Mom, you are my family. Family cares about each other and loves each other unconditionally. That is what you give to me. It means so much to me I could have a life with you, where I am surrounded by love, joy, and peacefulness. It is the opposite of how my life used to be, so I am grateful. It means everything to me. I am now living a genuine life based on love. We are a wonderful family!"*

10
HANNAH AND SKYE, TWIN LOVE
BY CATHE AND LARRY, HANNAH AND SKYE

Hannah

Skye

Many years ago, we adopted a pup named Sophe, a beautiful peach and white Shih Tzu–Maltese mix. She was the sweetest little dog, loving, happy and healthy, until one day she began having seizures and suddenly transitioned. Losing Sophe broke my heart so much that I didn't want another dog, but Larry did. Larry knew that adopting a new dog would help us heal. Within a week of Sophe's transition, we searched for a dog similar to Sophe and found 3-month-old twins, Skye and Hannah. We immediately fell in love. When we went to meet them, both dogs came running, Skye chasing after Hannah. It was easy to see how bonded they were and how much they loved each other. We brought them into our forever home that same day.

It was confusing for us to experience both joy and grief, but the pain of losing Sophe subsided with the pure joy of living with Skye and Hannah. Hannah said, *"We both knew that we could help you with grief. We knew you would want to cuddle us because we are so cute. We wanted to share our love to help you. Our love helped your hearts to heal."*

Now, every time we come home, we are greeted with love. It is so wonderful to see the two girls dance and twirl with joy.

Hannah said, *"We make you both giggle, and that is healing. That transforms grief by bringing in love for and from the new pet."* Skye said, *"All the same for me too. We knew we were ambassadors of new love to help you both. Do you see that? It may have felt fast to you, Mom, to adopt a new pet. Know that everything happens for a reason. We were there at the right time, and Dad knew the timing was right. You must follow your instincts as Dad did. That's magical!"*

We both learn from Hannah and Skye as we observe them and understand what they feel and need as individuals. They teach that the relationship with each other comes before all else. They show a tremendous depth of love and that the intricacy of their souls is as complex as it is with people. It takes a lot of openness, caring, and observation to know someone, including your pets.

Skye shared, *"I believe we are together in this lifetime because you are open. You are open-minded to seeing the loving guidance we provide you. I feel your inner fear helping you see it. I experience your peacefulness too, and you reflect that back to me. It is a great relationship, a partnership."*

Skye and Hannah love to take walks. Skye said, *"I encourage you to stop and smell the roses when we pause and appreciate the little things you experience on a walk."* Now that she is older and has arthritis, Hannah is sometimes initially reluctant to walk. Hannah's initial reluctance changes to enthusiasm once she walks. She teaches that if you are feeling reluctant to do something, do it because you will have the time of your life!

Skye and Hannah appreciate every moment of life. They express this by rolling in the soft green grass and being excited to see and smell new things. Hannah says, *"Does that make you appreciate life more too, Mom and Dad?"* We confirm it does. Life is so much richer with a pet.

Hannah says, *"I am grateful you adopted Skye and me together. We are a complete family, being all together. We are a match made in love. We all complement each other with our personality traits. This is fun and makes our family strong."*

Skye explains, "*I want my parents to understand my purpose in life is teaching unconditional love. Our relationship is filled with unconditional love. When you look at me, I am a constant reminder of unconditional love because the family relationship is based on that kind of love. I know that you both love us no matter what, and we love you no matter what. That is unconditional love!*"

"*Having human parents is a divine connection,*" said Hannah. "*My relationship with Skye is special because we are both dogs, but knowing that I can have a loving relationship with two human beings has changed my perspective on life. Feeling your love and how much you express it has changed my perspective on what love means. Love is limitless!*"

We know that Hannah and Skye are a family match made in Heaven. We believe previous pets help you find your new one. Sophe loved us so much and knew we were grieving. Sophe guided us to find Skye and Hannah so a new love would fill our hearts. When animals cross the rainbow bridge to Heaven, God sees and knows the pain of the human heart. Heaven cared so much; we received twins!

This may be a lesson for anyone whose heart is broken by the loss of a dear pet. It is hard to lose someone you love and choose to love again, but making that choice is wise. New love helps you heal and provides love to a pet who needs it. This is what Skye and Hannah did. There is a deep connection of love with animals that is profound and everlasting.

11
TEACHINGS FROM MY TWO YOGI'S
BY KAREN TAKAYAMA AND YOGZ/YOGI

Yogz

Have you looked back on your pets' lives to see the impact they have made on your own life's growth? My love and appreciation for my furry family grow each day as their love helps me navigate my life and share more love with others.

Before Yogz (Yogi-2) came into my life, I had another cat named Yogi. Yogi taught me so much. He was a huge orange and white tabby cat, tall and handsome as cats go. Yogi was very sociable and adventurous. Yogi could wander a mile away and find his way home. I knew he wandered far and wide as well-meaning people would call me via Yogi's pet tag to let me know where he was, and they would keep him until I came to pick him up.

Yogi and I had a connection. I would tell him, "I am going to leave for work, so if I let you outside, you need to come back in 30 minutes, ok?" I would open the sliding glass door to let him outside, and I would get myself ready for work. As it would near the time for me to head off to work, I would send Yogi an intuitive message to come home because I had to leave. On cue, Yogi would come trotting into the house and back into my room where I was getting ready! I'd always be amazed and let him know what an awesome cat he was. We would do the same routine at night before going to bed, except on Friday nights. Friday night was party night in the community, and I would give Yogi the choice of coming in now or staying out all night. On some Friday nights, he would choose not to come in. On those nights, I slept on the couch waiting for him to come to the glass door, and I would let him in at 3 a.m. or some early morning time. I let my Mom in on our routine, and she would just laugh, not believing that cats could communicate in this fashion.

Yogi would connect intuitively and through body language too. For instance, he would stand by his litter box and naturally get my attention. I would ask him why he was standing there. After a few times with no response, I would walk over and realize his litter box needed cleaning. I would laugh and get to work cleaning his box. Another time he was standing in the kitchen, and I again asked him what he was doing. He would just stand there like a Master teacher, the strong silent type. So I walked into the kitchen and noticed his dry food bowl was empty. I would laugh and fill it full. Intuitively communicating through body language is quite effective.

Yogi taught me a lot about love. I could feel my heart open more and more and heartfelt compassion filling my whole being. The warmth he showed me, how he interacted with the neighbors who all thought he was such a sweet cat. He spread his love everywhere. One time I went looking for him outside, and he was hanging out with the other cats in the neighborhood. They were all sitting in a circle. It was so remarkable like they formed their own community circle!

Yogi enjoyed being in high places, like the king of his empire, on top of buildings or climbing on top of people's cars. One day, a neighbor asked me if Yogi was my cat. He explained Yogi had jumped on his car, then onto the roof, and looked down into the window at his dog! He laughed and said what a bold cat he was. Yogi was full of love and so fearless.

At that time in my life, I had a very busy work and school schedule. I left him for a couple of days which turned into weeks, with my Mom. When I went to visit, Yogi did not look well. My Mom said he had stopped eating, so she took him to the vet, who diagnosed Feline Leukemia. I immediately took him back to care for him, and he improved for a time, but he started not eating again, and he was not well. After a time, I took him to the vet for assisted passing. But Yogi realized this and jumped out of his carrier, and scurried away outside. He paused, turned to look at me, saying goodbye. I told him I was sorry, and I asked him to come back in three years when I could spend more time with him.

Fast Forward Three Years

My friend called to inform me she had a litter of kittens. She invited me to adopt one. At that time, I felt I couldn't. She kept the kittens for a year, sending me photos. I visited her the next year, and the kitten jumped into my lap! My friend exclaimed, "Wow! She rarely does that, nor even comes out to see visitors." I petted the young gray and white cat as she pranced around. The next day my friend called to say the kitten was not getting along with her other cat so she would have to take the kitten to the shelter. My friend suggested she would rather I take her. My friend brought the kitten to me, crying tears of gratitude. As she brought the kitten inside and let her out of the carrier, the kitten ran out and into the bathroom. I went into the bathroom, sat on the floor, and said in a soft voice, "You are fine." I looked at her, she looked at me, and as I gazed upon her face, she looked like Yogi! This kitten was a female, though. I said to the kitten, "If you are Yogi, give me a sign." I saw a shimmering light coming down from above that went into her body, and her body shook. When I saw that I gasped! Was I seeing things, or was that a divine sign?!

Yogz said, giggling, *"I feel so joyful with you! Wasn't that cool that you recognized me on a soul level? It is magical, a genuine gift of Spirit. I believe you appreciate me as a teacher because you are learning so many things from me. I jumped into your lap as a sign that I chose you. Even though you did not pick up on it right away, it still worked out, and you received that divine sign."*

I thought of keeping the name Yogi for this new kitten, but it got confusing at the vet. I changed her name to Yogz as my previous male cat was Yogi. Yogz (female Yogi) continues to teach me a lot about love. She is the cuddly kitty that I always hoped for. I can cuddle with her; she talks to me and loves to be brushed.

Having a male and then the female cat has taught me a lot about masculine/feminine qualities. Yogi, the male, was very strong and adventurous and taught me he knew how to take care of himself. He shared those qualities and taught me to be the same. Yogz, my new female kitty, enjoys being pampered like most women. She talks all the time, wanting to be cuddled and groomed. Not having kids of my own, my feline "kids" have helped me to appreciate the differences in male and female qualities. Yogi taught me to be an independent woman, enjoy life, and take risks; Yogz is a role model for feminine self-care and delicate love and compassion. What a blessing to have them both in my life!

Yogz said, "*Karen, you are showing people you can notice with your eyes the signs and messages that a pet gives. You do not have to hear your pet talk; you can recognize their body language and behaviors as communication. That is important.*"

It is funny because Yogz is a girl and definitely more vocal and loves to talk. Yogz replied, "*I do like to talk! I am young and alive.*"

I feel like both cats have allowed me to understand love, to open my heart more, allowing love to be felt internally and externally. A pet's love is unconditional. "*That is a big purpose for pets!* Yogz said, "*Pets are helping people to embrace more love. You are engaging more with me, petting me more, talking to me more, showing your love more. You have opened your heart, and that is beautiful!*"

Yogz is also a protector, assessing all visitors like a watch cat. Yogz will either stay in the room or run out when we have visitors, depending on what she feels. Yogz adds, "*I know if a visitor loves animals or not and base my location on that. I leave the room if the visitor does not care for pets. I can read hearts, so if a person loves animals, that feels good, and I stay. If another person dislikes animals, I leave. I base my decision to stay or leave on how the visitor feels in their heart about animals.*"

As an Acupressurist, I provide acupressure sessions for clients. Sometimes Yogz will lie on a client, supporting them. She bases her behavior on what she feels from the client. Yogz is a healer too! Yogz giggles, "*Isn't that cool? I get to work with you! I love taking part in that with you.*"

I noticed that sometimes Yogz gets jumpy, so I am wondering if she is feeling something. I am not sure if she gets scared or skittish from wild animals outdoors. I usually pick her up and hug her to let her know everything is all right. Yogz said, "*It feels very grounding at home and very stable there. What I felt was the outdoor activity of wild animals. Animals are empaths, so I do feel a lot. So sometimes, I have a startling reaction to what I am feeling. I love your reassuring hugs!*"

Yogz continues, "*It is all about love for us, Mom. That love comes in many forms and feelings. I am supporting you to experience all those forms of love, with the biggest and brightest being unconditional love. When you can unconditionally love yourself, then you can share more love with others. Love helps everyone to be less judgmental and more compassionate. I base our relationship on the highest form of love available from our Creator. That love is never-ending and undying and flows through our hearts and souls."*

Love and Blessings to you!

12
BUTTERCUP THE LIFE COACH
BY DARCIE LITWICKI AND BUTTERCUP

Buttercup

Love comes into our lives in surprising ways, and meeting my horse Buttercup was no exception. At the time I met Buttercup, I was professionally training horses. Heidi Vanderbilt, the owner of Lucky Pup Ranch, had hired me to gentle a small herd of Arabian horses that had been raised on the ranch. In that small herd of horses was a seven-year-old bay Arabian mare that was more aloof than the rest. She often made her way to the back of the group of horses, and I would end up working with her last. I did not know at the time if it was because I worked with Buttercup last or because of some other reason that she was often on my mind after leaving each training session and even in-between sessions.

I looked forward to my weekly sessions at the ranch. It was with gratitude that I worked with the horses in such a peaceful and beautiful landscape. There were rolling grass hills and rugged mountain backdrops as far as my eyes could see. Each of the horses received about 30 minutes of handling during their sessions. My first task was to use my body language to move them at liberty in various directions at all gaits in a round corral. This work included the horses learning to stop and come to me in the center of the round corral for a little rest and petting. I would then either rope them with a lariat or place the loop over their head and onto their neck to teach the horses to give to light pressure. The pressure would be released immediately upon them giving in to the pressure even a little. This would help the horses be more confident and understand how to work with people. We practiced with future equipment like saddle blankets, saddles, and bridles, which would lead to the horses being ridden. From there, I would teach them to stand and be haltered and then follow light pressure on the lead rope to become comfortable being led.

I loved every horse had their unique individual physical abilities and personalities. I was often feeling tired by the time I got to the last horse, Buttercup. However, once we got in the training pen together, I felt re-energized. She was very smart and did not need to be shown what I was asking of her multiple times. Once she understood one lesson, I learned I needed to move on. Slowly, her fun personality showed, and she often had me laughing. For example, she would nicker at me out of the blue, and when I laughed, she would do it even more, or maybe louder. One time, Buttercup knocked over a plastic barrel and began rolling it around the training pen with her nose. The more I laughed, the more she rolled the barrel.

After about a month of working with the horses at the ranch, I noticed that when I arrived, Buttercup would be at the front of the group of horses in the holding pen where Heidi kept them on training days. She would nicker and whinny at me when I stepped out of my truck. When I left the ranch at the end of the day, Buttercup would remain at the pasture gate watching me drive away, even though she was turned loose in the pasture and the other horses headed up the hill for water. I would see her in my rear-view mirror still standing there as I drove up a steep incline and rounded a curve that took me out of her sight. I noticed a twinge of sadness each time I drove away and felt sure that Buttercup felt that way, too.

I knew in my gut that I was becoming attached to Buttercup, and the connection was building between us. As the group of horses progressed in their gentling training, it was time to take them one at a time to my place to start their riding training. They needed to come to my place to work with them daily instead of once per week. Riding training required me to be focused and disciplined to help the horse be successful. Buttercup was the horse I picked first because she was the furthest along. She was also more focused compared to the other horses. I could continue traveling to Lucky Pup Ranch to work with the rest of the horses once per week for a while more, but Buttercup was ready to move forward.

Buttercup said, *"I knew from the moment I was in the presence of Darcie that we were supposed to be together. It was a feeling I had, and I could tell that Darcie felt that too. It was so beautiful. What was cool is I knew I could show Darcie how smart I was by learning things quickly, which would pique her interest in me more. She could see who I am because we are like soul sisters."*

When it was time to drive to Lucky Pup Ranch to pick up Buttercup and bring her to my place, Heidi informed me that

Buttercup had never been in a horse trailer before. Horse trailers go against a horse's instincts because these trailers are dark enclosed spaces. A horse must trust in the person asking them to load into a trailer because they would not naturally allow themselves to be trapped in a confined space. This fear is due to horses being prey animals, and being trapped would not allow them to run away from a predatory animal. I arrived extra early to have time to teach Buttercup how to load and ensure her that she was safe. Before haltering her to bring her over to my waiting trailer, I got everything ready. Then I walked Buttercup up to see the trailer. She sniffed it for a moment and investigated the open door. I stepped into the trailer to show her it was okay, and to my surprise, she walked right in with confidence. She stood in there with me for a bit and then completely relaxed. It was amazing!

On the drive, I stopped once to get out and check in with her, and she was calmly standing in the trailer, much to my relief. Once we arrived at my place, I opened the trailer door, and she walked out as if she'd lived here all her life. She greeted the other horses with a soft nicker, sniffed noses, and went into her pen without a care in the world. It was on this day that I knew Buttercup and I were meant to be together. We were heart-connected.

Buttercup says, *"We share this strong connection of love with each other. I knew I needed to show Darcie in a big way, that I wanted to be her horse and that I was choosing her by walking calmly into that trailer and walking off that trailer the same way and making myself at home in her place. I love being here!"*

After a couple of weeks of riding her in her training sessions, I spoke to Heidi about Buttercup becoming my horse. Heidi was a firm believer that Arabian horses choose their person and had already felt that Buttercup had chosen me quite some time ago. I was very excited to get Heidi's approval to keep Buttercup. We worked out a barter deal of me providing training services for her other horses in exchange for Buttercup. Buttercup replied, *"I'm so happy that Heidi helped to bring us together!"*

I have learned so much from Buttercup over the years. One of the biggest things she has taught me is to practice mindfulness to be more present. When we were first riding out on the trail together, she was often reactive and would jump sideways or bolt forward suddenly. I felt tense when she did that, and it was jarring to my body, too. I knew I had to figure out how to stop tensing up because horses can feel every muscle on a rider's body, and having my muscles tense added to her tension.

I started paying close attention to what was happening when Buttercup was startled. I noticed that my mind was usually off somewhere else, and I knew horses were very present in every moment. When I was not present, Buttercup felt she was on her own to make herself feel safe because she couldn't trust that I would be in the moment with her to help her when something was scary. By paying attention, I began working on breathing and being centered and balanced in my body while riding on her balance point. This helped me move with Buttercup instead of tensing up. The breathing also helped me relax, but when my mind wandered, she would startle or speed up. The more I worked on this, the less she was startled. Before too long, she went along quietly on the rides for the most part. If Buttercup startled a little, I noticed that when breathing, my body stayed in balance with her, and then we would come back from the startle together all in one smooth motion and in balance, which helped us both be calmer. Becoming more mindful has helped me in my work with horses and life immensely.

Learning mindfulness has offered me a way to help and support my coaching clients by teaching it to them within our sessions. I primarily work with women in one-on-one coaching, group coaching, and workshops. As the owner of Silver Heart Ranch, where I work as a certified coach, I integrate life coaching with Equine Assisted Coaching. Silver Heart Ranch is an encouraging place for women to come together with horses and nature so that they can explore their inner selves more deeply within the coaching process. Horses have the inherent ability to respond to people in a way that is honest and mindful of how the person is showing up. From this interaction, people can reflect on what the horses' responses mean to them and apply those to the coaching they are engaged in. This creates a true experiential process that is profound and beneficial for self-growth.

"Thank you, Darcie, for learning mindfulness," Buttercup replied. "It truly supports your clients—horses model mindfulness to help to learn from it. Horses are a bit calmer and peaceful inside, which is a place you too can find inside yourself through mindfulness. I understand the human mind likes to chatter a lot, so learning mindfulness is important as it helps you feel calmer inside."

Buttercup continued, "I love co-coaching your clients with you. I feel like your human perspective and coaching helps your clients, and then my horse's perspective helps too."

I always consider my horses as coaching partners. Horses reflect to the client what they feel is coming up inside them that they may or may not be aware of. Buttercup coaches through body language. One way she does this is to gently walk away if she feels the client is not aligned. A person needs to authentically allow their emotions to match up with how they are behaving for Buttercup to be comfortable with them. If the client feels sad inside but puts on a smiling face, Buttercup will instantly reflect the incongruence through her behavior. Once the client takes some time to process what is going on within them and engages with me in making some changes or shifts to become more aligned, Buttercup will let them know they are on the right track by walking over to the client and interacting with them. This is one of many ways that horses can teach us more about ourselves.

Buttercup agrees, "I LOVE doing that work! How cool is it that Darcie understands how horses support people in this way, which helps her and her clients."

I appreciate Buttercup has a sense of humor. Sometimes, if a client touches her somewhere ticklish, she will make a soft nickering noise, making the client laugh, which breaks the tension. If there are obstacles inside the arena, Buttercup might knock them over or push them around the space, just being silly. When she does this, she shows clients that while coaching is serious work, it can be fun, and people need to play too. It melts my heart when I see her play and share so much joy. I know how much it means to others too, when they receive this message from her.

Buttercup and my other horses trust me to ensure that the clients who enter the work arena will be respectful of them and will not hurt or be angry with them. I support my clients with processing any of those feelings before entering the horse area. We do this in our one-on-one coaching work. Then, right before they enter the horse arena, we do a few grounding breaths. This gives my clients more practice so that they are more likely to remember to ground themselves before other events in their lives outside of coaching. Buttercup replied, *"I do trust you because we are so connected. You know people well and can sense what they need. The work you do inspires the right people to come here, so I trust that, and I am grateful for that. I love co-coaching with you and appreciate you."*

Buttercup said, *"Darcie, I appreciate your big, wide, open heart and all the love and care that you share with me and my herd mates and your other animals. Your clients benefit too that you are a kind and generous soul. I love you dearly!"*

I am humbled repeatedly by the way Buttercup shows up for my clients and me. One day Buttercup and I were working with a client in our horse and owner relationship coaching program. This is where I work with the client and their horse to cultivate a deeper relationship. The client engages with me for their personal growth, and then we take the outcomes from that work out to put it into practice with their horse. Buttercup and I went out on a trail ride with the client and her horse so that they could feel more comfortable and connected. After a few miles, we came to where bright pink plastic tags and ribbons were hanging on a temporary plastic fence. The gas company had put it there to mark an area they were working on.

The client's horse did not want to walk through that area because he was afraid of the plastic items blowing in the breeze. The client became fearful and frustrated when her horse would not move forward. She was forgetting to breathe and relax, which is something she had been working on. I reminded the client of this and talked her through her exercises to help her relax. This would help her horse relax because all the emotions would come down. Once things were calmer, Buttercup stepped forward and took the lead by walking through the area. Then, as she got partway through, Buttercup looked back at the client and her horse, telling them to come on and follow her. The other horse took a few tentative steps, checking out the plastic ribbons by sniffing them, and the client kept breathing. After a couple of moments, the client and her horse walked through the area calmly and confidently. The other horse saw it was okay, and the client learned it was better to be calm and allow her horse a few moments to think and relax.

Buttercup said, *"This story shows I am a leader. I lead other horses to teach them. I am an old, wise soul that knows a lot, and so is Darcie! I am grateful to help other horses too. I am eternally grateful to you, Darcie, for these opportunities to support others."*

I've learned so much from Buttercup. She has taught me to slow down and take my time with things. She shows me I do not have to push through everything at once; I can work with small pieces one at a time and relax. I push myself hard, and Buttercup taught me I do not need to do that. I love her spirit and her big heart. She is such a special being, and I am blessed to share my life with her.

Buttercup said, *"What I most want Darcie to know about our relationship is how much I appreciate her. Not everyone will look at what their horse might try to show them or teach them. Darcie is open to it, and she embraces it to help bring change to her life, which is all humans need to do. Whether you have a cat, dog, horse, bird, turtle, or hamster, all animals communicate with you and support your life. Darcie sees all the beautiful things and is open to learning from me. It is a beautiful gift of service she provides with her love. I'm thankful that I can live this life with her. I cherish it. I am grateful, and I love you, Darcie!"*

13
KIARA THE SHINING STAR
BY TANYA LOCHNER AND KIARA

Kiara

I had just adopted a Dobermann called Rapha (meaning my healer) from a high kill shelter. He was the most loving soul that helped me heal my loneliness. I could see he was lonely during the day when I was away at work, so I got him a friend.

Since I was a little girl, I was smitten with border collies from watching countless episodes of a show called Lassie - a Rough Collie that helped save the lives of humans in various adventures. This inspired me to find my own little star.

As I entered the Border Collie Rescue center, I immediately noticed the dog playing soccer by herself. Barking at the ball, she had intense eyes and focus. Later in life, I would discover that one of my superpowers is focus. I could help others with focus, so it was no coincidence that I felt drawn to this girl. I named her Kiara.

Kiara says, "We are Soul family. You and I belonged together. When you came to the center and saw me, you knew in your heart. It was a soul-to-soul connection. I was calling out to you, and you brought me home. I am eternally grateful for that."

Little did I know that besides my gift of focus, this amazing collie would reveal to me my soul's purpose here on earth - to help others unlock and achieve their full potential.

Kiara says, "I helped you open your heart to see what your purpose was and how brilliant you are that you saw that. I know you were sad when I crossed the rainbow bridge. I am with you now as your four-paw guardian angel."

Being a border collie, Kiara had a high energy drive. I started doing agility training with her. This is where dogs run an agility course with obstacles such as jumps, ramps, and tunnels. I remember our first lesson where the trainer asked what our goals were - I innocently said to get her over one small jump. Little did I know Kiara would do multiple courses with high jumps and ramps. She even competed a few times and got her Canine Good Citizen bronze medal. Boy, did I underestimate her potential!

I started noticing that she had a particular talent for herding. I know it is a breed instinct, although not all collies do this gently or well. I never found sheep for her to herd, which has always bothered me. I felt I did not help her use her untapped potential as a herding dog. I could never give her that opportunity.

She was always the light of my life, which is what the name Kiara means. She would always be close to me and even helped me connect better with other people. I would take her with me on camping trips, and even though I'm an introvert, she would happily greet others and support me in starting conversations I would otherwise never have had.

She passed away at a good age after ending her support role of guiding our new Australian Cattle Dog, Ecko, and rescue Border Collie Jett. She had beautiful mothering energy, which delighted anyone who got to know her, young and old.

You're probably wondering how she helped me find my soul's purpose. I decided later in life that I was ready to be an entrepreneur and help others by coaching them to build a successful business. I grappled with what I stood for and the big message I was meant to share with the world to make a difference. I know a lot of entrepreneurs get stuck in that space, too.

I had done a branding photoshoot, and Kiara was part of that wonderful, exciting journey. I remember thinking, "She will always be a part of my business now."

As I was going back and forth with figuring out how I'm meant to best support others - the memory of Kiara's herding talent kept coming up for me. Initially, I held so much guilt over her not being able to fulfill that potential. I then realized that I could not stand seeing unfulfilled potential. Another "light" had gone on for me. I realized I could help others uncover and fulfill their potential!

How do I do that when I couldn't help Kiara do it? I questioned my purpose. Again, the unconditional love of this beautiful soul comforted me with her message:

Kiara says, *"Mom, do not have any guilt. Yes, herding is a breed trait. You did something much better and more fun, though. You took me to that agility training course, and I got to run it. The running of the course was like herding, so it was very good for me, and I enjoyed it. I am grateful you allowed me to do agility with you! I knew you were having fun too, Mom. We had fun together doing agility competitions. I could run as fast as I could through all those different obstacles. I was good at it and enjoyed it because I got to do that with you. I did not need to herd sheep; I had agility, a genuine gift of love."* Kiara's message helped me understand that there are multiple ways for us to fulfill our potential!

Kiara catapulted me into my soul purpose, helping me see I have a gift to see the potential in others and their business and help them. Kiara was like a social butterfly, always urging me outside my comfort zone. She easily connected to people, helping me to do the same. She taught me to get out of my own way. Today, I support entrepreneurs to identify what their potential is. I thank Kiara for that gift because she gave me the experiences that highlighted this for me.

Kiara says, *"All pets have a purpose. Our love is big and bright and beautiful, shining upon human hearts. Your heart was open to everything. I was showing you and teaching you. Thank you for embracing the teaching, plus all the spiritual messages I provided. It is so cool that you were open to that, that we shared such a powerful relationship. There is no deeper relationship of love, except in heaven with God. The animal/human relationship is built on such profound love. I am incredibly grateful for our life together!"*

Kiara continues, *"I just want you to know, Mom, that our relationship was special. Never have I had an experience where I have lived with a human being that embraced unconditional love as deeply as you do. You completely understand unconditional love and can express it to other people. I am happy to have played a part in that. What I want to say is that some people might take their pets for granted. I want to encourage everyone who loves animals to embrace and experience their love and allow it to uplift you. The more you enjoy your pet's love, the more you support others with love. More love, more love, more love is what this world needs!"*

I know Kiara is with me in spirit. I consider her my heavenly business partner. I am forever grateful for her loving heart. She will always have a special place inside my heart. The name Kiara in traditional Italian means bright star or shining brightly. She is my bright, shining star!

❊ 14 ❊
GRUNT'S FARM UTOPIA
BY SUZANNE ELLISON AND GRUNT

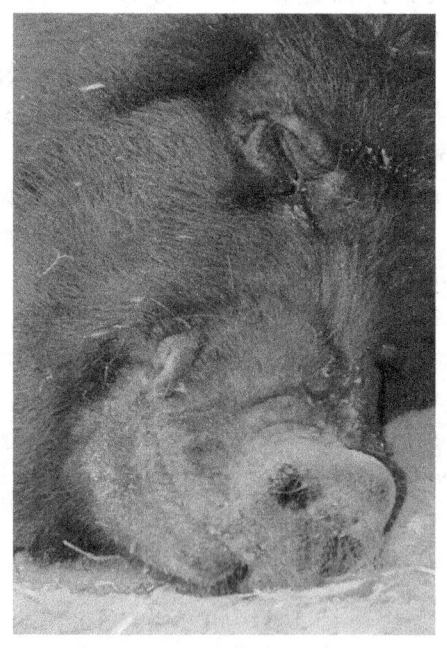

Grunt

From the time I was young until now, I'd always had a selection of pets. My pets included rabbits, dogs, cats, guinea pigs, gerbils, a monkey, goat, chickens, fish, parrots, budgerigar, big horses, miniature horses, and peacocks. Then there was Grunt, our pet pig.

My father was in the sugar industry and used his job as a way of seeing the world. We would move about every three years. As it was before the internet, it was not possible to keep in contact with the friends I made everywhere. Having pets helped to fill the gap of losing friends each time we moved.

I got married and went to live in the wide-open spaces of Zambia, Africa. On paper, it sounded amazing, but having never been a person to just sit around, I decided I needed to find something else to do other than just being a wife. I found the answer to my boredom in a recipe book. No one in the country, and Zambia is a big country, was making ice cream commercially. There was some horrible ice cream being made by the Dairy Board, but no one liked it. This gave me the idea to make creamy, smooth, melt in your mouth ice cream. Over 25 years, this ice cream became a national brand of Zambia, along with seven other dairy products I made and sold.

Now you might ask yourself, "What does making ice cream in Zambia have to do with a pig called Grunt?" The answer would be nothing, initially, but as my business grew, I thought it would be a great idea to get a few cows of my own, so I could supply myself with the main ingredients that I needed to make my products, such as the milk, cream, and butter. I bought ten cows, which, over 25 years, grew into a herd of 400 beautiful Jersey cows.

During this time, two daughters were born to my growing family, and nothing gave me greater pleasure than being with them and having all the pets and farm animals. But there was one pet that was missing. My daughters thought it would be amazing to have a pet pig.

We lived in a farming area, so there wasn't a shortage of pigs around, but I thought it would be nice to find a small breed of pig or a miniature pig if possible. I put the word out, and a few weeks later, I was told that a lady in the next farming community had "small" pigs. I contacted her, and she confirmed she had small pigs for sale. The next day I drove over to her farm, and sure enough, there in an outside pen were all these adorable piglets running around. I asked again if these were a small breed of pig, and she assured me they were, but as she had recently separated the piglets from the mother, I couldn't see how big the sow was. Not that we didn't have space for a normal size pig, I just thought that a miniature pig could stay around the house and be a pet and not outgrow being a pet and become another farm animal.

I came home with a small pig that fitted in the footwell of my car. Of course, the little piglet thrilled my daughters, who were already loving the piglet. The piglet was quite happy with all the attention.

We had the piglet for quite a while before any of us could think of a name for her. We quickly discovered that she was very "talkative" and would constantly grunt when she heard my daughters talking. If you spoke to the piglet, she would grunt back in response, and the girls would have a conversation with her. It seemed very appropriate to name the piglet "Grunt."

Because she was tiny, Grunt started life with us, living in our extensive garden. The miniature horses would come in and play with her during the day. The horses were quite cheeky in their own way. The doors into the house were always wide open. The miniature horses would come into the house and stand at the back of the couch looking for attention, along with Grunt, who being much smaller, and none the wiser would just come all the way in looking for the girls so that she could have more personalized attention. We also had dogs and cats who would come and go in the room, and the girls would bring their cockatiels out. All the animals got along so well.

It was amazing how all the different species of animals came together to enjoy life and have fun. The animals understood we loved them. Bedrock Dairy Farm was a beautiful place to raise my children and a wonderful environment for my daughters to grow up in.

As I mentioned, we had a large garden, and Grunt was free to roam around wherever she wanted. As she got older, she began making a mess by digging up the grass and the flower beds and making sand or mud baths everywhere. Because it was so hot in Zambia and we had to water a lot, we only had a small area of grass around the house where the girls could play and also to keep the dust down. Having Grunt going around digging up the garden because it was soft and moist was not working out. We decided Grunt would have to move over to the dairy.

There was a good supply of water within the dairy, and we could make her a permanent mud bath for her to wallow in. She would have all the cows and the young calves as company, and the girls would still be close enough to see and play with her every day.

I knew pigs were smart, but I didn't realize how smart. Grunt was so smart she figured out where the calf food and milk were and began chasing the calves away so she could eat their food. Grunt was shorter than the calves but had a much denser body, and she used this to her advantage to flip the calf cages over, letting the calves out and spilling all the food on the ground, which she would then eat in no time at all.

Having now learned where she could find a constant supply of food, Grunt made it her mission to wait till no one was around and then flip the cages, let the calves out who would go running off in different directions, and eat all their food. While pigs are very clever, I also learned that they are very stubborn and not so easy to train. So, unfortunately, we had to build her a large fenced-in enclosure to stop her from stressing the calves and eating all their food.

Provided the dairy workers were around, they let Grunt out, and she loved nothing more than to sit amongst the milking cows after they had milked them. At first, the cows found this disconcerting, as Grunt would literally walk amongst them and then just collapse next to one of them, grunting in absolute pleasure she could be one of them. She was so happy, but the cows couldn't care less. It was quite funny to watch this, and she never ceased to make us laugh.

As Grunt grew older, she grew into an enormous pig! I realized that she wasn't a miniature pig. By that time, she was as much a part of the family as the dogs and cats in the house. Grunt loved her wallow, and the girls would spend so much time just scratching her tummy with a stick. Whenever they stopped, she would grunt and grunt until they started scratching her again. The conversations they had were amazing, with the girls talking away and Grunt, grunting in reply. She loved the attention and always had the look of pure joy on her face.

Grunt did not ask for much but gave my daughters and me so much in return. There was lots of enjoyment and only a few headaches when she got out, unsupervised on occasions, but she never got up to too much trouble that couldn't be fixed. She was a very happy pig.

When my daughters went away to college in England, I moved there to be with them. My daughters continued to go back to Zambia to see their father for several years after they left and always came back with stories about Grunt, who was then quite elderly for a pig. She had grown into an enormous pig. In fact, she was so big that my youngest daughter could sit on her and not touch the ground.

Eventually, the day came when my daughters got a message from their dad to say that Grunt had died in her sleep and that they were going to bury her under her favorite tree by her wallow. She was such an amazing pig and a family member who will always have a special place in our hearts.

Grunt says, *"That was the happiest life on the farm. Suzanne, when you came to see all the piglets, I chose you, and you brought me home to your beautiful farm family. You gave my life purpose! As a small pig, your thought to treat me like a dog was brilliant because pigs are very smart. You treated me with respect in a loving, compassionate way. You gave love to all the animals on the farm, but I got to have a more special relationship with you. My relationship was closer with you and the girls than with the other farm animals. That is super-duper special! I began my life developing human relationships, then moved on to building relationships with the other farm animals. I could take the love you shared with me to the cows. This gave me the purpose of spreading love. Your human love was so big and bright. I took it to the cows, trying to make friends with them and help them see that. I became an ambassador of love!"*

Grunt continues, *"The entire farm was about love. You loved and cared about the animals. Even though you called the farm Bedrock, it was truly a Bedrock of love. I am grateful that I got to experience all these different relationships: human love, dog love, cat love, bird love, chicken love, horse love, and cow love. This has taught me that love is love, no matter the species."*

Farm animals taught me a lot. I always wanted to do my best and do what was best for the animals. We bring animals out of their natural environment and place expectations upon them. It is up to us human beings to look after animals to the best of our ability. Sometimes I feel like I might have let some of my pets down. However, when other dairy farmers would visit my farm, they were always so complimentary. One visiting vet even called my farm a cow hotel! It was not about the money spent in their care; it was about my passion for them and what the animals gave in return. Our ice cream became a national brand in Zambia!

Bedrock Dairy Farm was a pleasant environment for my daughters to grow up in, surrounded by those animals. My heart breaks for children that grow up without being in contact with animals. There is so much that animals can teach us, including compassion, respect for each other regardless of what species we are, and as humans, to look after the planet to the benefit of everyone.

Grunt says, *"Allow this story to be a role model for everyone. When animals on a farm are respected, cared for, and loved, success happens. When farm animals are treated indignantly, they do not want to produce, and the farm struggles. Bedrock Dairy Farm was a loving place where the animals were happy and good ice cream happened. I am eternally grateful to have been a part of that."*

🌀 15 🌀
KAYA THE ROLE MODEL OF LOVE
BY ANGELIE AND STACY O'BRAZA-PEREDA AND KAYA

Kaya

We first set eyes on our German Shepherd from a picture that Stacy's co-worker showed her. The co-worker knew we were looking for a dog, and we wanted a German Shepherd. She showed us a picture of a dog hiding in the bushes, looking frightened. Stacy came home and showed me the picture, and I just felt like we needed to save her.

Three six-month-old German Shepherds were dumped along a wilderness area to fend for themselves, two boys and a girl. The brothers were rescued after about three hours, but Kaya was terrified and hard to catch. Eventually, she was rescued too.

We met Kaya with Stacy's co-worker who volunteered for the German Shepard Rescue of Northern California, but she was scared and hiding in a bush in the parking lot. Regardless of her being so timid, we still wanted to rescue her. We fostered to adopt her, just to be cautious. The following weekend Kaya arrived at our home, still holding onto fear. She was so timid; she crawled around the house low to the ground, tail tucked in. We had to put trails of food on the floor so she could get to know our house and feel somewhat comfortable.

Stacy adds, "Angelie and I just sat there looking at her. And Kaya was looking at us. And we were like, now what? We had not had a dog for years, just cats, but always wanted a dog. Kaya was so scared we did not know what to do. We just looked at her, and she looked at us, and I just felt so much love from her."

Kaya also did not enjoy going in a car for obvious reasons. We took her to Starbucks for a Puppuccino. We had to lift her 45 pounds into the car. These types of short car trips helped Kaya overcome her fear of the car.

Kaya responds, *"I am grateful they rescued me into their family of love. I am grateful that Angelie and Stacy saw my picture, looked into my eyes, and knew I would be a good fit for their family. You both rescued me with your love because you saw how scared I was. Being abandoned in the wilderness with my brothers was a very traumatic and fearful situation. That is why I appeared so scared when you first met me. The power of your love was so big and unconditional. You recognized my fear, and you loved me anyway, and that love helped pull me up and out of my fear. That is a beautiful gift you have provided to me."*

Stacy says, "I feel like Kaya has helped me with my anxiety. She has opened a unique part of my heart. Because I love Kaya so much, she has shown me I cannot wait to have a child to love too."

Kaya helps me with anxiety, getting me out of the house walking her. She provides me with companionship as I work from home, so I never feel alone while Stacy is at work. It is nice to have Kaya with me. I can hug her when I need to, and that feels healing to me. She is a splendid companion who is super easy-going and chill. Kaya sleeps on our schedule. If we ever sleep in, so does she. Kaya also enjoys traveling with us on vacation trips. It is so cute to see her running around, loving the beach, seeing snow for the first time. She enjoys these outdoor adventures. Kaya has become very kind and sweet with other people and animals. It has been amazing to see Kaya overcome her fears to live a more peaceful, fun life with us.

Kaya, blowing kisses, says, *"I feel like I am a part of a powerful female team, having adventures with you. It is so amazing you both recognize what pets really do for their people. Love does open hearts! I want everyone to understand and see that pets are helping people to open their hearts. When you realize your pet is doing this, your life changes for the better. I want others to see that possibility in their pet relationships."*

Kaya likes everybody who comes over to visit, or she thinks everyone is there for her. Kaya says, *"I'm like the welcome party!"* It's cute to see our friends and family say hi to Kaya when they come over.

Stacy remembers, "One of Kaya's first trips was to Lake Tahoe. We went with our friends and their dogs. It snowed overnight, and there were about four feet of snow on the ground. We went outside that next morning to go sledding down the street. I started going down the street hill on the sled. I called out to Kaya, who then ran right beside the sled all the way down, smiling from ear to ear. It was so cute! She ran about half a mile with me, sliding down the hill. That was Kaya's first experience with snow, and now she loves it."

Kaya responds, *"That specific adventure that Stacy is talking about is the moment I realized my life was going to be fabulous! I realized how fun life was going to be with you both."* We noticed that something changed in Kaya after that. She began wagging her tail all the time and just seemed happier like she finally trusted us. Kaya continues, *"So here I am, a dog abandoned and dumped, having deep-seated anxiety. They knew I did not want to have that in my life with another human being ever again. When you both showed me and taught me I was safe with you, I realized I could trust you. I had the self-realization that I was in the right family. I was getting what I wanted—a family of love, adventure, and fun. Woo hoo!"*

We went on vacation to the Russian River in Northern California. We stayed in this pretty place that had a huge backyard on the river. Kaya loved it! She would run around and do her own thing. She even dug up a toy buried somewhere. Kaya always looks so happy when we travel. I always wanted a dog to travel with. We feel safe with her. We have gone camping, and she's our little protector, even though she's a scaredy-cat. Kaya replies, *"It is my size and breed that commands respect, but I have a teddy bear demeanor."*

I appreciate how caring Kaya is with other people and animals. She has been around kids and is very sweet. My friend was pregnant, and Kaya was respectful, not jumping on her at all. It is like Kaya senses when she needs to show caring. She is motherly and gentle. Kaya is a very thoughtful dog.

Kaya replies, *"Thank you both for your loving words. I see those qualities within myself. I feel it is important not to live in fear but to live in love. I am grateful you see my loving, compassionate, motherly qualities because that is what I choose to express out into the world. I choose to be gentle with others. I understand myself and my size and that some people are afraid of big dogs. I want to come across as gentle and kind so that people can trust me. At the beginning of my life, I did not trust human beings. You both have my trust. I know that if you trust someone, then I know I can trust them too."*

When we go for a walk and see little dogs, Kaya will sit down politely because she can tell the little dogs fear her. So, she sits and waits for them to walk by, sometimes even lying down on the ground.

It is like she is saying, "Look, I'm nice and patient. When you are ready to come up to me, I'm ready to play." It's so sweet.

"*My relationship with Angelie and Stacy,*" says Kaya, "*is based on true unconditional love. They saw my fear, and they expressed unconditional love for me. Now I can express that unconditional love to them and others as well. The love that we share is an outstanding example of unconditional love, compassion, and caring. All people and animals can do this with each other, making life better, happier, more balanced, free, and fun. If a pet is afraid or they misbehave, it is because of fear. Your unconditional love in that situation is healing for your pet. I am a good example of that and a role model for my family. My family members provided me with unconditional love. That helped me to shift out of fear and live a peaceful, fun, happy life. It is the same for everyone. When we are kind to each other, care about each other and have compassion for each other, then unconditional love is powerful. It is healing. Our family relationship is like a beacon of unconditional love shining out into the world. I want everyone to see it. I want everyone to embrace it and receive it. Understand that you too can give love unconditionally to other people and all animals, including your pet, who might live in fear. When you give unconditional love freely to others, it means you do not judge their unacceptable behaviors, but you approach them with compassion, care, and love, like my family did for me. Know that unconditional love like that changes lives. My family relationship is showing everyone how life can be lived on the highest level of love.*"

Kaya continues, "*That is what life is about, and I am eternally grateful for my family and the relationship of unconditional love we share. Most people take unconditional love for granted, or they do not even think about it. I am asking everyone to think about it, to embrace love and give unconditional love to others because that will make this entire world a better place forever.*" That's how we feel too. Kaya is a true role model of love!

16
MY ROYAL AKITAS
BY EMILY KANE, OKAMI AND KIMI

Okami and Kimi

When I first saw his face, I knew I had found someone very special that I had to meet. I had only recently found the desire to step through my grief of losing my Labradors to love again. I had two Siberian Huskies at home, but they were so different from my Labrador Retrievers, whom I had lost several months before (within 90 days). The five of us were a pack, but it was very clear we had lost something special from our home without them.

I missed their excited 'welcome home' greetings. Maybe it was our collective grief, but we had somehow parted ways with the Siberians. My Huskies, aka my 'cat-dogs,' sat in chairs in their 'lair' and barely showed interest in activities. I longed for our snuggles and play. I was not sure which breed or gender would become our new pack mate, just that I was ready to find him/her.

I searched across rescues, breeders, and stores for months. There were more dogs than I had even considered. Although adorable, they all still seemed unremarkable. The only thing I knew about our prospective pup was that he/she would have to be a good family fit for my existing dogs, children, and grandchildren. I had almost given up when I stumbled across a photo of a new Akita pup from the local pet store. I looked up the traits, potential ailments, temperament, etc., of the Akita. I had forgotten the dog depicted in the movie *Hachiko* was an Akita. Perhaps in my research, there were a few breed qualities I had overlooked because of the movie.

I had lived in Kami Seya, Japan, when the *Hachiko* movie was being filmed in Odate in the late 1980s. I continue to feel a deep fascination for this country steeped in rich traditions dating back for millennia. The Japanese use naming conventions for their native dog breeds to reflect the part of the country from which they originate and then "Inu" to mean dog. In this case, Akita Inu is from the Akita prefecture, in the mountainous part of northern Japan.

I called the store immediately to see if this lop-eared puppy was still available. Something about him seemed to capture my soul. When they said yes, I asked if they could hold him long enough for me to drive across town. In my elation, it occurred to me I forgot to ask how much adoption would cost. As I was driving, I called back and - there was a sticker shock. I could have turned around, but I was transfixed on meeting this puppy that had so resonated with me through his expressive eyes and confident posture. There was something almost magical about him. I had never seen an Akita in person before meeting Okami.

When I arrived, he was not responding like all the other puppies. He did not jump, play, or lick—he stood there looking at me with an air of independence. That was confusing because I expected something much different. Perhaps because of his pricing—he did not want to get his hopes up or, as I suspected, he was sizing me up as we locked eyes. When the clerk checked in with us, I heard myself saying, "We need puppy things; it's been a long time since I had a pup."

Okami giggled, saying, *"When you saw my beautiful face and looked into my eyes, you knew I was the one for you. It was true! It thrilled me to meet you. That you adopted me into your family was a dream come true. Kimi joining our family was also another gift to me."*

It did not take long before reality sunk in, and I heard protests from the Siberians about Okami. I had never experienced this behavior before. My previous '4-pack' seemed to fall into step easily. At first, I attributed it to how I had improperly introduced them, but then there was clearly more going on. When I got everyone into the house, the Siberians retreated behind their chairs and rarely wanted to be in the same room with Okami.

We selected the name Kuro Okami Kuma in honor of the breed's Japanese heritage. The Akita also has the nickname of "bear." Okami's face was very similar to the shape of a wolf. Collectively, his long title translates to Brown-Wolf-Bear. Another translation of Okami is "great God," which could be equally fitting because he seemed to be an ancient, wise soul. He understood all his training - he was brilliant.

Over the next few weeks, I let everyone become organically acquainted. Yet, it was obvious I had to bring in a behavioral specialist to remedy the Siberian's hurt feelings and to train Okami with acceptable pack manners. As an excited new pup parent, I could not wait to tell everyone about my smart new boy. These conversations were often met with warnings and alarms about Akita's overly protective and aggressive breed behaviors, and the safety of small children, etc. I was ecstatic that Okami was widely accepted and complimented by our daycare facilitators, mobile dog groomer, veterinarian, and trainer. I was repeatedly told that he had a solid temperament and good social skills with people and the other animals.

People consider Akitas territorial and protective. They were bred to be very large and powerful animals with scissor-like jaws used mostly for hunting the Japanese black bear, deer, and other big game and blood sporting. Over the centuries, there have been many changes to the Akita dog line, including breeding them with other larger, more muscled, and powerful dogs like the German Shepherd, St. Bernard, and Mastiff for sport and creating laws protect them from harm.

"In 1680, Japan's fifth shogun Tokugawa Tsunayoshi, known as the Dog shogun, came to power and created laws that forbade cruelty to dogs and the Akita dog breed. He is also responsible for issuing the Law of Compassion called the Shorui Awaremi no Rei, which levied punishment for harming dogs." (Tokugawa Tsunayoshi, Encyclopedia Britannica).

During World War II, they used these deeply loyal Japanese hunting dogs for the war effort — eaten or used to line military coats. By the time of the Japanese surrender in 1945, only sixteen Akita dogs were left in the country. The breed's survival was primarily because of the passion of Morie Sawataishi, as documented in the book *Dog Man: The Uncommon Life on a Faraway Mountain.*

Okami was not bothered by the behaviors of the Siberians;

however, I felt he needed someone like him, so when he was four months old, I investigated adopting another Akita. The Akita breed is known to have aggression within the same gender. I was nervous about bringing a little girl into a pack of males. It highly surprised me that there were no Akita in Colorado or our surrounding states. I found only one Akita breeder that was in Pennsylvania, and that is how I found a pretty, fluffy girl that we named Kimi, Kimyko, or "noble one."

Kimi was flown by plane in a crate to Colorado. She cried and cowered from our very first moments and was reluctant to be touched at all. It was clear the flight was traumatizing for her. Her crate was a mess, and she was shaking. I hoped that getting her cleaned up and pampered a bit would help to calm her anxiety. My neighbor, Lexi, held her in a clean blanket to comfort her until we could get her to our local dog wash facility for a bit of a puppy spa day, new accessories, and bedding. I told her she would never have to go back into that crate—and she didn't. We wanted to ease her fears and let her know she was safe.

When we got home, and Kimi met Okami, it was friendship at first sight. Kimi seemed to feel safe around Okami and followed him everywhere. After weeks, she rarely wanted anything to do with people. Okami was always ready with kisses and a playful attitude, while Kimi preferred to sit on the outside and observe.

Kimi replied, *"I had a rough start in life. You brought me into your house of love, Mom, and I am forever grateful to you. I thank Okami for all the gifts of love he provides each day."*

Although Okami and Kimi are both Akita Inu—they have completely unique personalities. Kimi will not jump, and I'm not sure if she even knows how to. Trying to get Kimi into the car can be a challenge. Okami jumps in and leads the way because he cannot wait to go to doggie daycare. When they return home, Okami bounds for the back patio to announce he has arrived. Kimi will follow him, but then she backs away. Okami has almost human eyes, and Kimi is a diva with glorious beauty marks on each cheek. After grooming, she pulls Okami's bandana away from him because she is the only 'pretty girl' and loves being told that. Kimi shows her pride by wiggling her curled tail like it is her glowing crown jewel.

I look into my dogs' expressive eyes and tell them how beautiful and smart they are. I believe in socialization, and I see the difference it makes my dogs. If we can let go of preconceived notions about breeds and treat animals well, then pets are happy. Every animal deserves loving care. By expanding my awareness, I notice what my dogs are trying to tell me. I sense what they need by their behavior patterns and body language.

Their personality differences teach me many things. Okami is cool and laid back but also playful like a puppy. He also has a tremendous sense of humor. When Kimi misbehaves, and I ask the doggies who it was, he stretches out across the floor as if to let Kimi tell on herself because she always shows remorse. Okami also jumps onto my uncle's bed and tries to sit on his face if he sleeps too late. When Okami likes someone, he leans on their legs as if to tell them he chooses them.

Kimi is more of an observer of life. She will find a safe space from which to observe, such as the top of our staircase. Yet, she will reach out and ask to be scratched in her favorite places. She tells me what she wants by getting my attention, then walking me toward whatever she asks. Kimi also has babies she likes to carry around in her mouth as she sort of growls to herself. It makes me wonder if she protects her 'stuffies' like she wanted to be protected as a puppy. I can see myself in both of my pups because while I am very sure of myself with some people, it might take me a minute to warm up to others.

There was an incident that resulted in Kimi puncturing my finger. It was an accident, but Kimi hid beneath my bed in fear. I had to coax her out by telling her how much I loved her and knew she didn't mean to hurt me. Kimi says through grateful tears, *"I felt so remorseful because I understand it was an accident, but I was afraid you would get angry with me. That's why I hid because human beings can get angry with their pets. I expected that to happen. You showed no anger, only love. Your love is so powerful it just drew me out. That is the power of love, and I thank you for that, Mom! Because you treated me with loving-kindness instead of anger and frustration, it helped me to trust you. Most people would get angry, but look at how beautiful you are, Mom! You chose love. You chose to love even when I hurt you. You chose love, and I wish everyone could do that with their pet."*

Kimi then waxed poetic, saying, *"I wish to express the importance of treating your pets and all animals with love and respect. It is love and respect that brings out more love from your pet. It can be easy to get frustrated with your pet's behavior when things go wrong. Animals can have fear, causing misbehavior such as chewing on things, hiding and shaking, barking aggressively, or biting. All of that is FEAR. I want people to know that it is fear behind the misbehavior. It is not that a pet is trying to be mean or naughty. Animals do not behave like that. When your pet shows fearful behavior, you can be like my Mom and be loving. It is love that is greater than fear. That is my message to the world.* **Love is greater than fear.***"*

Okami says, *"Mom, the way you lead with love—that is all people have to do with animals—***Lead with love.*** That is my message to the world."*

"We are in this life together as a family for learning and growing," said Okami. *"Most of all, for love because you are a shining example of love and how human love can change a pet's life. When a pet experiences love and care from their human, the pet respects that. Pets give unconditional love to inspire humans to do that as well. Mom, you are an expert in unconditional love for all your pets. Thank you! Kimi and I are very grateful to you. May we be a part of this loving family forever."*

Kimi adds, *"I completely love you, Mom, and I want you to understand what you have done for me. You've brought me from a place of fear into the warm embrace of love. Your warm embrace of love means everything to me, and you're helping me overcome my fears. I am grateful that you come from love and embrace me with your love. I am forever grateful to you."*

If people have lifestyle expectations of a pet, they should find a pet that shares those traits. Still, that is only the beginning because every pet is also an individual and member of your family with their unique contributions and personalities.

. . .

References:

Sherrill, Martha. *Dog Man: The Uncommon Life on a Faraway Mountain.* Penguin Group, 2008.

Britannica, The Editors of Encyclopedia. "Tokugawa Tsunayoshi." Encyclopedia Britannica, 19 Feb. 2021, https://www.britannica.com/biography/Tokugawa-Tsunayoshi. Accessed 15 August 2021.

17
HARPER AND HOPE, THE WISE OWLS
BY CHANTAL, HARPER, AND HOPE

Harper

I have been rescuing and rehabilitating animals my whole life. I studied nature conservation in college & have always had a passion for animals. Four years ago, I started my own company with the vision of bringing my dream to life. My big dream is to open my own Wildlife Rehabilitation Center.

I've rescued and released many animals in my life. I do not believe in keeping wild animals captive. If they are capable, healthy enough, and able to defend themselves, wild animals must go back into their natural habitats, preferably where they were originally found. In some cases, where they have injuries or illness making it impossible to release them, I will then create the space they require and ensure they have the correct care needed. Should I not be able to give this to the wild animal, I will consult with other organizations and find the best solution for the animal.

Harper gets to steal the show. He is a Spotted Eagle Owl I rescued as an owlet (a baby). Four years ago, I got a phone call from my cousin. One of her friends was working at a road construction site in Africa. She received a phone call from her friend telling her they had found two owlets on the ground and wondered if she knew anyone who could help. The owl's parents were nowhere in sight. The owlets had been there about two days with no luck of going to a rescue center. I was called and agreed to help. By the time I had arrived at the site, one of the owlets had passed away. The sibling was just sitting on the ground, a tiny owlet maybe a week and a half old. The owlet could fit in the palm of my hand.

On inspection of the owlet, he was extremely fragile, just skin and bone. He was covered in maggots and ants, pretty much on his death bed. It was such a harsh thing to see. It was horrible, but I knew I needed to decide if he could be saved. I gently picked him up and just felt that he was a fighter. I rushed the owlet home and gave him some high-protein food and electrolytes and treatment. I decided that if he made it through the night, we were good to go. If he did not make it through the night, we knew we had done the best we could for him.

Most wild animals are scared by human beings trying to care for them. This owlet was different. He sat quietly, allowing me to attend to his needs. It was kind of like he was saying, 'okay, do what you need to do.' He let me handle him, so I cleaned him up a bit. The owlet had been in a high-stress situation, so we mainly addressed food and fluids and kept him warm. Every two hours, I fed him. I looked at him and said, "You have fought this hard so long. Come on; you can do it."

We named the owlet Harper, and he did survive the night. The next few days, he was feeling better, eating and drinking well. He was behaving more as an owlet should, which showed us he was feeling better and on the mend. We provided him with mice, and he chugged them down as fast as he could.

Harper says, *"Chantal, you are my angel. You rescued me; you saved me. You saw something in me, and I felt your love and knew I would be okay. I knew that you would take care of me and help me in any way. That is why I sat there peacefully for you. I felt an immediate trust with you."*

Harper had a wound around his beak, with a puncture wound on top of the nose and a hole underneath the beak. That is an extremely sensitive area for owls. He also had an eye injury, and his eye was swollen shut. The depth of that hole underneath his beak seemed never-ending. He had maggots coming out of his nose and wound; I wondered how I could get them out. I sat with an earbud, pulling them out of the hole one by one. There must have been over a hundred maggots inside his wound. Harper patiently sat there the whole time, even though it was painful. He let me do exactly what I needed to do. From that day forward, Harper's health improved, and he got stronger. He did, however, lose his damaged eye even though the wildlife veterinarian and I did our best to save it.

Harper says, *"Mama, I can feel your loving and caring heart! That spoke to me when I was so scared because love overpowers fear. I knew that the love you were expressing towards me meant that you would do the best for me, and you did. That is why I was a good boy for you and allowing you to help me like that. Most wild animals would not sit peacefully. I realized that those maggots inside of me were trying to kill me. It was a battle going on between your love and their nastiness. You patiently sat there, pulling them out of my nose and wound, one by one. You showed them who is boss!"*

As Harper grew older, we realized that there was optical nerve damage done by the maggots to his healthy eye. The eye had no visible signs of trauma, but behind it was damage, so he lost most of his vision in his good eye. Because of this, his flight is not that great. Harper tends to like walking wherever he goes. He will fly up to sit on something, though. He has integrated into our family well. Harper has befriended all the rescue animals in our home, the dogs, the cats, the chickens, the horses. He loves to cuddle.

Harper has a very distinct personality. I have always envisioned him having a posh English accent. He is a prim and proper guy who has taught me so much about life's adversities and what you can face. He has overcome so much!

Harper replied, *"Here I am today; I am happy and healthy. I may not have a perfect owl body, but I am super duper happy in my family. I give you my heartfelt, deep, unending gratitude from my soul to yours for what you have done for me. You not only saved my life, but you also saved my soul. Before you rescued me, I sat on the ground, not caring about living anymore. It is like God heard my prayers, and you showed up. You are my angel."*

Harper showed us that with no vision, he still wanted to be a part of our lives. I felt he must have freedom and not be restricted, so he walks freely. He would walk along the walls, floors, grass, trees, and tap like a blind human would as if he was mapping out the area. This is how he learned about his surroundings. Harper will come and find me to be a part of whatever I am doing. Harper says, *"I use echolocation like other animals. Since my eyes are not working, my hearing is amplified and has become my primary source of information."*

About a year into Harper being in our lives, I came home from work, and he did not look well. I felt something was not right. I asked Harper, "What's going on with you?" and he just fell over! I grabbed him and rushed him to the vet. As I got to the vet, he started to seizure & his heart stopped. I was standing in the middle of the vet's waiting room, sobbing my heart out, with this little owl in my arms. The vet came out and brought us into the consulting room. The vet looked at me, checked Harper, and the next minute Harper took a big breath! I was stunned.

Harper spent a few nights at the vet and was very unhappy and did not like it. He was on an IV drip and refused to eat. I knew Harper was not happy, so I told the vet that I felt Harper needed to come home. I felt that being home in his environment, he would feel better and more inclined to eat. The vet agreed because Harper was so stressed out.

We got home, and I had Harper in my hand. As I walked into the house, he opened his wings and wrapped them around me, laying his head on my chest. We stayed in this embrace for about 15 minutes; he was holding me so tight. All the animals in the house came and stood around us. I sat Harper down on the floor; the animals sat around us in a circle. It was a happy family reunion. As we sat there, I offered Harper food, and he ate with everyone watching. His wings wrapping around me and hugging me is something I will never forget. It is one of the most special, memorable, loving moments we shared.

While the vet could never pinpoint what was wrong with Harper, we suspect he may have had a Vitamin D deficiency. Although Harper spent a lot of time outdoors, it was winter, so he chose to stay indoors more often. Even though he got sunlight through the house windows, they block a lot of the UVB, which is very important for owls. I would take him outside, and he would walk back into the house. Now Harper spends more time outside as we have built an outdoor enclosure onto the owl room for him and our other two rescue owls.

Harper says, *"Do you realize what you did for me again in taking me to the vet? I heard your wails of grief and knew I needed to snap out of it. My heart did not stop completely but slowed down too much. I willed myself alive for love. Wasn't that like a miracle?! It is always Chantal to the rescue for me!"*

Harper is teaching me so many things through our deep, strong connection. The day that Harper came into my life was the day I decided to open my own company. I had just left my old job. I was stepping into a world I knew very well, but not the business side. My whole life, owls have taught me things will always work out. Harper showing up made this business incredibly significant for me. It boosted my self-confidence in stepping into the unknown.

Harper was a sign that I was on the right track and doing the right thing. I realized I could also start thinking about the rehabilitation center too. He shows me that through life's adversities, your attitude will govern where you go. You can choose to have a positive attitude or see the challenges as negative. I choose to see challenges as things that need to be worked out. Harper's choice in choosing to live shows us that you can choose to have a positive attitude in life's adversities.

Harper smiled, saying, *"That is my big lesson for you! You saw the adversities I went through and overcame. If I can do that, you can do whatever you pursue."* That is something Harper shows me regularly. He is so accepting of whatever comes his way, good or bad. He takes everything in his stride, living life with dignity and respect.

Harper says, *"Human beings think there are good and bad situations based upon how you feel. A situation is just something you move through. If you can set aside the idea of good and bad, you deal more peacefully with the situation you face. Even though it may hurt physically or feel uncomfortable, you can just move through it. You always come out on the other side."*

Harper is a wild owl, and what a wise teacher he is! I believe all animals are here to teach us. They survive through life's adversities and understand the life cycle and how it works when it comes to standing together. My animal family teaches we can live together in harmony.

I have three rescued Spotted Eagle owls named Harper, Hunter, and Hope. Hunter had rat poisoning, and Hope had emotional & physical wounding. Other owls I have rescued have been released back into the wild. It's a strange and wonderful thing that another beautiful owl enters my life around the same time every year.

Hope's Story

Hope

Hope's story is one of redemption. As an owlet, Hope hated human beings. She was a different challenge from Harper. When I received Hope, she was older than Harper. I could feel her anger, feeling as if Hope had lost her purpose in life.

Hope was found by a woman who was walking her dogs. She saw some kids having a big commotion, throwing stones and screaming and shouting, so she approached them to see what was going on. It was then that she saw the owlet, about three weeks old, on the ground. She was tiny but very feisty and scared.

I got the call and picked her up. When I met Hope, I began crying because I could feel what she felt. I envisioned her fighting these five kids. I could also feel her anger, wondering why anyone would torment an animal, let alone a baby animal. I took her to the vet, where she was very stubborn, not wanting to eat, take medicine, and did not want us near her. She had eye injuries and wounds from the stones that were thrown.

Hope was so different from Harper. Where Harper was patient with me, I had to be patient and calm with Hope. I had to imagine how she felt so defenseless, put myself in her position. I took her home determined to help her.

Upon examination, she had severe damage to one eye, but the other appeared okay. I needed to apply eye drops to Hope's eyes, and she fought me every step of the way. Sadly, we were unable to save her eye, and she lost it completely. She did not want anything to do with humans. She did not understand that I was trying to help her. She would full-on attack me. I would tell her I was only trying to help her, but Hope did not understand.

I told Hope I wanted to tell her story to help others learn. I wanted to protect her from harm and help her if she would only allow me. I explained she could help educate other humans on how to help animals. Hope felt her purpose as an owl had been taken away from her, and she blamed humans for that. It took a long time to earn Hope's trust.

Hope says, *"My name Hope explains who I have become. That is my name, and that is who I am now. Chantal gives me hope, so I am hopeful. Chantal gave me my purpose in this new family. Hope is my new identity in my family. It is not the purpose I was born with, but it is a purpose that is important. Thank you, Chantal, for never giving up on me. I was fighting against humans because of my experiences. It was hard for me to trust you. I had to forgive those other people so I could find this hopeful piece inside of me. You, Chantal, helped me to do that by not giving up on me. That is an important lesson for everyone. When you love someone, do not give up on them, even if they fight against you."*

Hope was a challenge. We now have a special relationship and trust each other based on love. She trusts me more than anyone else. It is important not to give up on those you love. Slowly but surely, she came through her adversities. Today Hope is calm and happy, a true testament of redemption.

Hope has progressive vision loss in her good eye and is now learning from Harper how to move around. Hope and Harper became friends. Harper tells Hope, "*Even though your vision is dimming, you can use your hearing to support you. You can recognize family members' voices and use echolocation.*"

Hope teaches us that harsh journeys require forgiveness. She has shown that forgiveness and love are the way. If you continue to give love, it can help situations evolve into love which will grow so that the negative becomes positive.

Hope replies, "*Thank you for sharing my story. I had a lot of emotional pain, and you understood that. You developed greater patience and chose not to give up. The greatest gift of all is the unconditional love you give to me each day. People can get stuck in emotional pain, so it is important to treat everyone with love, no matter how upset you feel. You always come from love, Chantal, and I love you. Your love healed me into love. A human's unconditional love is powerful. I encourage everyone to embrace their inner love and express it and use it to help others.*"

Harper concludes, "*I am happy to support Hope too with her healing. Wild animals do talk with each other and with other animals. We have cats, dogs, horses, and chickens, and we all communicate with each other. In our family, we are loving, living, and growing together. Thank you, Chantal, for being an animal advocate!*"

18

THE FAB FIVE PLUS ONE
BY SUZANNE THIBAULT

Never did I imagine we would have five pets in our family. We are a family of animal lovers. Our lives literally revolve around our crazy household filled with cats and dogs who uplift our spirits. Animals have a way of climbing inside your heart and setting up residence there. Once you make that heart-to-heart connection with a pet, there is no turning back, and your family grows by leaps and paws.

Allow me to introduce the Fab Five: Odie (Dachshund Terrier Mix) and Abby (Rat Terrier Mix) were adopted from the California Animal Shelter Friends Inc. in 2009 and 2013, respectively. Lily (Purebred British Shorthair Cat) joined our family in 2014; Jack and Luna (Tabby Cat siblings) were found outdoors and rescued in 2016. We never planned to have five pets, but together they have formed the Fab Five, who are all so fabulous as they surround us with their love every day. Our plus one, Watson the Rebel Hamster, rescued from death in 2010, is now in pet heaven.

The Fab Five work daily in my personal life to teach, support, counsel, and make me laugh. It took many years before I realized that they were teaching me life lessons. It takes an open heart to notice an animal's loving guidance. As a Pet Communicator, I share my unique relationship with each of the Fab Five, including their impact on my life, in the following chapters. May you find your pet's guidance to inspire you in life. When you realize your deep, spiritual relationship with your pet, your life becomes magical and inspiring.

19
ODIE THE PERPETUAL PUPPY

Odie

You know how pet adoption works. You scour the internet looking for adoptable pets. As you browse through the photos, you lock eyes with a four-legged cutie pie that steals your heart. You make an appointment to meet them, and your heart lights up with joy. This is how we discovered Odie, our currently 12-year-old Dachshund Terrier Mix rescue. He was a very handsome puppy who was quiet and hand shy.

Odie settled in nicely with our family as our first dog. We discovered he loved to take apart stuffed animals. So, we purchased him a durable, stuffed toy Dragon. It was love at first sight for Odie! He cuddles with Dragon, licks his Dragon, chews on his Dragon, sleeps with Dragon. Eleven years later, this toy is still available to purchase, thank goodness. We have gone through many different Dragons over the years as his favorite toy. Oddly enough, it was Dragon who introduced us to Odie's vocal variety.

The traditional game of fetch had us tossing Dragon through the air with Odie running and catching the toy midair. Then Odie would shake Dragon back and forth while growling loudly – really loudly! Every time Odie plays with Dragon or another toy, we get the growling noise so loud it drowns out the TV. He still does this at age 12. It is quite a comical experience. It delights us to know Odie is enjoying his Dragon so much that he squeals with glee. That play growl is what makes him a perpetual puppy while sporting his gray muzzle.

Most pets calm down as they age, but Odie is endlessly stuck with a puppy mentality. Odie says, *"Yes, I am a perpetual puppy because I am modeling to embrace your inner playfulness at any age. Life is meant to be enjoyed through play. Play is important and healthy for you. It lifts you up as you play and laugh with others. There is no better way to embrace your play than to make some vocal noise! My play growl expresses how I feel. You might interpret the noise as growling, but I am expressing laughter and joy as I play, saying Woo Hoo! Lighten up, have fun, and play."*

I also found it interesting that Odie has been so attached to a toy Dragon for his entire life. There has been no other favorite toy, just

Dragon. He has played with other toys but always returns to cuddling with Dragon. Not just any toy dragon, it has to be the goDog Plush Dragon dog toy.

Odie explains, *"As a puppy, I felt abandoned by my mother and siblings. That was hard for me as I felt so alone, and my heart ached. When you adopted me from the shelter, it was hard for me to bond with you at first. Introducing me to Dragon, I realized this was a toy I felt comfortable with. This toy didn't yell at me, and it squeaks loudly like me. I bonded with the Dragon, thinking of it as my friend. Everyone needs a friend in life who does not judge them and only loves and cares about them. Dragon feels safe to me. Life is less scary when you have a best friend."*

Odie loves to play with his Dragon. Every time I see Odie playing this way, it reminds me to play too. In this way, Odie is helping me stay young at heart. He sees how I'm feeling inside, then ramps up his perpetual play to make me laugh and lift my spirit. It is hard to stay feeling down when Odie's around.

Odie is a foodie. Each morning he wakes up at the same early time. I drag myself out of bed to feed him. He is always bright-eyed and wagging tail as I yawn through my fogginess. Odie bounds out to the kitchen in excitement. He waits patiently as I prepare his food. As I walk towards him with his full bowl of yumminess, Odie performs a happy dance in anticipation, spinning and jumping front paws upward. He truly reveals joy in this eating ritual that makes me giggle. His perpetual peppiness is inspiring!

Odie says, *"I am a foodie! Haven't you noticed I am not a picky eater? I will eat everything. Food smells delicious to me. Maybe I have a heightened sense of smell or something. I get excited because I am grateful! My happy dance is to show my gratitude for the meal. My behavior speaks volumes about expressing more excitement about the small things in life and stop taking things for granted. I challenge you to perform a quick happy dance before your next meal and see how you feel! Be grateful for the food that nourishes your body. Healthy body, healthy life. It is important to be grateful and celebrate the small stuff."*

Odie's vocal variety also emerges when we prepare for a walk. Walking is Odie's favorite sport, running a close second to napping during the day. When Odie hears the crinkle of the plastic poop bag coming out of the draw, the excitement begins. Happy dance time! He gets so excited he starts squealing loudly like an exuberant toddler. Not just one squeal, but an entire parade of loud squeals as we walk towards the door. He then screams a squeal extra loud in delight, as if he is saying, "Hurry up and open the door!" His vocal squeals hurt our ears.

"*Oh, how I love to take walks outdoors!*" says Odie. "*So many smells, so much beauty. I love feeling the breeze on my face as my ears flop up and down. Are you aware I actually trot and not walk? My bouncy trot walking expresses the pure joy I feel inside. When I pause to smell, I am reading the neighborhood news. But my pausing also sends you a message. Slow down and pause to enjoy the sunlight upon your face, the cool breeze in your hair, the sound of the tree leaves rustling above you. Making a connection with nature is healing. Stop overthinking and slow down to enjoy life.*"

One of the first things Odie has taught our entire family is patience. Odie loves to stand outside, sniffing the air, barking at nothing. We will ask him to come inside, and he will just stand there, staring at us. When he was younger, we got frustrated. Now we all understand he is teaching patience. Odie still does this behavior today, even though I have explained we have all learned the lesson of patience. I asked Odie why he keeps repeating his lessons for us.

Odie explains, "*Everyone needs a friendly reminder sometimes. Human beings are easily distracted. I notice you all get distracted, especially by your cell phones. The lesson of patience is important. It helps you develop the ability to tolerate delays without getting upset. That is something you can use in every area of life! You may not have noticed that I also model patience and tolerance every morning when I await my morning meal. I do not sit there and growl at you in impatience as you prepare my meal. I do a happy dance in anticipation of the good things to come! Tolerance is an outcome of patience.*"

Odie follows my husband, Mike, around everywhere, as he is Odie's favorite. This is an act of love, as Odie has a strong bond with him. Odie sees Mike as the pack leader, so wants to follow and observe everything he does, even in the bathroom! While this behavior is irritating, Odie does have another reason he does this. Odie leans on Mike for support and feels anxious when he's not around. This became clear when Mike and I took a short overnight trip. Our adult daughter stayed home with the Fab Five. Odie's anxiety peaked, and he was barking at everything for hours on end, suffering from separation anxiety.

Odie remembers, *"I feel safe when Dad is around. I follow him around because he is in charge. I like to lean on Dad as he makes me feel safe. My separation anxiety is related to an experience I had as a puppy. As a newborn puppy, I looked to my mother for food, protection, and love. Too young, I was abused and then taken away from my mother by human beings, winding up at a shelter with a sibling. When you are with someone who helps you feel safe, you cling to them like glue. Being removed from my mother and being abused by humans, I developed mistrust of humans. Feelings of abandonment are real for animals. It has been hard for me to build trust. Your love has shown me I can trust you."*

I have previously written about Odie's early abuse in my first book, *Animal Wisdom Tales-Messages of Love from Pets and Wild Animals*. I will briefly describe it again here so you can understand his behavior. Years ago, while meditating, Odie showed me intuitive pictures of himself as a puppy being kicked in the chest every time he barked. That abuse created PTSD-type fear inside him, resulting in mistrust in humans and overreaction to loud noises. Odie's separation anxiety was on a high level of PTSD-type reactive fear. It is through pet communication and supporting Odie to forgive the abusers that he has healed. While he no longer barks aggressively, he still has a few anxieties, such as separation anxiety, that bother him. Odie is taking medication that supports his inner peace. But whenever we take a trip, Odie's separation anxiety ramps up. Odie truly feels most comfortable with my husband's supportive love.

Odie is the bravest dog I have ever known. The puppy abuse, trauma, and anxiety with PTSD that he suffered have taught me the biggest lesson of my life. Animal misbehavior does not happen because a pet is a jerk or revengeful; it occurs because animals can have traumatic, emotional wounding. He also taught me the depth of an animal's emotional range. Animals feel pain as deeply as we do. Most importantly, Odie has taught me that pet misbehavior is not meant to frustrate us; their emotional wounding fuels the misbehavior. Emotions influence pet behavior.

Another lesson that Odie has taught me is that even if you are struggling in life, you can always stop and smell the roses and do a happy dance to lift your spirit. Choice is one of the most powerful tools we humans forget we have. We think we have to live a certain way, deal with the cards dealt to us. Odie's teachings have taught me to choose to change with intention, shift my perspective, and seek inner peace. These are all things I seek in life.

When I gaze into Odie's eyes, I look into the eyes of God. Odie's unconditional love and lessons are God's handiwork upon my life. I have learned to love unconditionally because of Odie's misbehaviors. I have learned patience, tolerance, and understanding. I have learned to look for the bigger picture in all situations. Odie has helped save my soul, leading me into the arms of the Spirit's love, protection, and guidance to lead my life. Your pet is doing this for you too.

For years I spent my early life struggling with indecision and self-doubt. I would make a decision, then second guess it. I would get frustrated, thinking I had made the wrong choice. Then I would face another decision and be right back on the hamster wheel, second-guessing and frustrated. This put me into a state of anxiety and then into depression. I stopped making choices because it felt overwhelming. I was not enjoying life. Odie could sense that inside me.

What muddles up choices and causes indecision is emotions. You can feel like you do not deserve it, feel emotional turmoil in making an important decision, not knowing which way to turn, afraid to make a wrong choice. That was me for many years. Indecision kept me stuck in a rut. Some people can take a risk and make difficult decisions, moving forward in life. Others like me get stuck. It can be hard to choose something positive when you are feeling uncomfortable emotions and self-doubt. I have had to learn to step over fear.

Odie taught me that the power of choice meant I could choose something better! Second-guessing and self-doubt would creep up, but I would look at Odie, which reminded me I could make the empowered choice to step over fear. He had to do that himself in choosing to trust us to care for him. Odie helped me learn to overcome fear and self-doubt by using my intuition to guide me in life.

Odie's presence in our family has challenged me to be a better person. I am forever grateful to him for his unending teaching, love, and support. Odie replies, *"I am grateful for my family who loves me with no judgments or conditions. They just love me!"*

20
ABBY THE WISE ONE

Abby

Abby is a Rat Terrier mix, a small bundle of big love who is my best friend. When I first noticed her photo on the California Animal Shelter Friends website, I just fell in love. As a puppy, Abby weighed only two pounds. When my daughter and I met her at the rescue facility, Abby stood confidently looking at us, smiling, wagging her tail. I loved her the moment our eyes met as she melted my heart. I admired her personality as a fun-loving, small dog with a big attitude. We adopted Abby and brought her home.

"*I remember that day; I was so excited!*" said Abby. "*I, too, knew we were destined to be together. I saw your soul shining bright love to me, and I recognized you. We are soul family."*

Abby entered our family as our second dog, four years younger than Odie. As a puppy, she looked up to her big brother. She would follow Odie around, and she learned all of his bad behaviors. Imagine having two dogs standing in the backyard, noses held high in the air, sniffing and barking for no reason. Whenever Odie would react in fear to noise or another person, so would Abby because she learned this behavior from him. This was very frustrating, making me wonder if Abby had been an only dog, would she have a more balanced life?

Abby replied, *"At first, I feared Odie because he was so much bigger than me. But I soon realized he was a big teddy bear holding onto lots of fear. Yes, my life might have been different if I did not have Odie's behavioral influences; however, I never felt the fear he did. I was showing Odie how silly his fears are by mimicking him. He never quite caught on."*

Odie's fear of noises, smells, and strangers caused Abby to react, but more gently. Sometimes she would cower and physically shake in fear. This was not the same dog I had met as a confident puppy. It was very frustrating that Abby would lose her self-confidence because she witnessed a lack of self-confidence that Odie was modeling through behavior. I had asked Abby about it. That is when we decided that agility training could help her build self-confidence. It was something she and I could do together without Odie.

Abby lives in perpetual happiness, with pure excitement for life that I envy. At that time, I suffered from anxiety, depression, and low self-esteem. Abby was able to see a better part of me, a part she was encouraging me to emerge and express. She placed a leash of love around my heart, determined to lead me forward out of my limiting beliefs and into personal soul truth and alignment with love. Abby was helping me tap into a part of my heart that I was unable to access myself.

"Just change your perspective to change your life," said Abby. These are the wise words she spoke to me one bright summer day when I was feeling irritated. My emotionally weary eyes gazed upon hers

with complete understanding. In her eyes, I could see the possibilities, and I just did not understand how to change my perspective when all my mind wanted to do was react negatively to everything. I sat there feeling frustrated and told her, thank you, not knowing what to do next. What Abby was asking me to do felt impossible. I tried endless positive affirmations, but my perspective never improved. This is what happens when you are deeply anxious and depressed; everything seems hopeless. Abby counseled me, *"There are many ways of changing your perspective. Do not be so hard on yourself. Love holds the answer."*

I was able to sign up for dog agility training near our home. Abby was excited by that news. She wanted to do agility training to build her self-confidence. Abby exclaimed, *"Yes! At that time, it was MY plan to do agility training with you. Did I have a secret agenda? You bet. You were the one lacking self-confidence."* She was right.

Dog agility is a sport where you lead your dog through an obstacle course, working together. Courses usually have about 14-20 obstacles, including tire jumps, seesaws, ramps, pause tables, weave poles, and tunnels. These are the obstacles Abby, and I started learning in the beginner six-week course.

Abby was the smallest dog in the class, and she shook in fear of being around strange dogs and people. I felt nervous too. I calmly reassured her that this would be fun. The first obstacle introduced was tires lying flat on the ground for the dogs to walk through. Abby handled that just fine. Next came running through a hard-sided tunnel with a clear view out the back. She trotted right through it to me on the other side with a smile on her face. We were off to a good start, and I could see Abby relaxing and getting in the groove. Abby states, *"I was not shaking in total fear, more like shaking in excitement with a little fear! I could also feel your nervousness, which made me nervous too."*

I soon realized I had to work on my self-confidence as Abby's partner. I was used to sweetly calling Abby, but the instructor told me to toughen up, stand in my power, and firmly speak the commands. My heart sank as I realized I needed to build my self-confidence alongside Abby. Abby just smiled and said, *"Now you know why we are here. We will both build self-confidence together!"*

The second class was not a fun experience. The instructor introduced a blind tunnel for the dogs to run through with a closed end that opened as their body moved through it. When Abby's turn arrived, she walked up to the opening and stopped, peering inside, only seeing darkness. She refused to budge as I called out to her excitedly to urge her forward. She looked at me with fear in her eyes because she could not see the light at the end of the tunnel. As an empath, I could feel her fear, her indecisiveness. She was frozen in fear. I was stupidly embarrassed as the other dogs were able to navigate the obstacle. My inner critic began beating me up with negative thoughts.

On the ride home, Abby said, *"I am showing you what you hold inside. You are frozen by fear; you are not moving forward on your dreams, and you do not see the light at the end of the tunnel. I am modeling this to you for your greater self-understanding so you can choose to change."* I cried tears of inner pain as we drove home. It can be hard to realize what is holding you back.

My tiny but mighty Abby did not really lack self-confidence. She was teaching me about myself. She was using her empathic abilities and reflecting to me how I was feeling inside. The shaking fear she showed me through her behavior was her empathic expression of *my* inner fear. Abby was an emotional barometer to my soul. I marvel at the depth of her love! She has kicked my spiritual journey of personal healing into gear. I was now determined to change, understanding how Abby was supporting me as my counselor.

Abby replies, *"This is what most pets will do for their humans if only people would take notice. We pets adore our human family and want them to lead a happy, healthy life. Because animals are empaths, we can feel how you feel and express that in hopes you will notice our loving guidance. I taught you this Suzanne so you can bring this gift to light for other animal lovers."* Thank you, Abby! You are the light in my life.

It can be challenging to look inside yourself and change. Living with Abby's exuberance for life inspired me forward. I wanted to view life as she did, without a care in the world, stepping over fear, having fun every day. Abby makes me laugh with her antics. I can tell she is happiest when she makes me smile and forget my worries. I appreciate the counseling she provides, but it has taken a while for me to understand the depth of her loving guidance.

The biggest gift of love that Abby provides to me each day is her wisdom. She has taught me so much about myself that I was afraid to see, gently guiding me to overcome my fears to live a more peaceful, happy life. That is a true gift of unconditional love. She sees and feels what no longer serves me. I realize this is also God guiding me too, so I choose to change.

Abby says, *"Are you ready to step into the truth of who you are? Mom, you are a shining example of Spirit's unfailing love, a beacon of hope to others who struggle, a role model in changing your life for the better. Take what I have taught you and share it with others so they, too, can step into living a life that has purpose and meaning. I love you!"* That brought tears to my eyes.

It is time to listen to pets as they are messengers of Spirit. The fact that both animals and Spirit possess and provide unconditional love to you speaks volumes! The next time you gaze into the eyes of your beloved pet, feel God's love inside calling out to you. That is the gift of grace your pet provides.

Abby replies, *"Our relationship is a strong bond of love that can never be broken. I do speak Spirit's wisdom upon your heart. Embrace and enjoy it!"*

21
LILY THE PURRING, PRECOCIOUS PRINCESS

Lily

LILY THE PURRING, PRECOCIOUS PRINCESS

Never had we ever thought about adopting a purebred pet. Our family is more focused on those pets in need at shelters. Something interesting happened that caused us to have a change of heart.

The first cat we ever brought into our family was a tiny, orange tabby kitten named Rory. He was a gentle kitten who loved to cuddle. He lived with Odie, Abby, and us for three months before passing away from Feline Infectious Peritonitis (FIP), a fatal viral disease. The vet believed Rory had contracted that virus as a feral kitten. Our hearts broke deeply at losing Rory.

My daughter began looking for kittens online without telling us. Two days later, she sent me an email at work with a picture of a cute little lilac kitten. I took one look at the kitten's beautiful face and saw Rory's face superimposed over it. This was an intuitive sign from Rory that this little kitten was right for our family.

The little lilac kitten was with a breeder in Grass Valley, an hour's drive away. She was not available to adopt yet. We had to wait a few weeks until she was older. In the meantime, I spoke to Rory using pet communication to ask about his passing. Rory explained that his tiny body could not fight off that virus, and his body organs failed. He explained he was coming back into a new healthy body – the purebred lilac kitten. My heart skipped a beat at that information. My mind reeled. Can pets really come back to us? According to Rory, yes. I asked the Holy Spirit for the truth and learned that animals do have the option to return to us in our lifetime. Their love is so big and bright they are motivated by love to do this. If it is in a spiritual agreement between all souls, the pet can return. This was mind-blowing information that lifted my grief away as I learned this spiritual truth.

A few weeks later, I drove to the breeder in Grass Valley to pick up Lily, the lilac British Shorthair kitten. Much to my despair, the breeder lived in an unkempt house with cages of kittens stacked everywhere. Lily was in one of those cages looking scared. This was not how I thought breeders cared for animals, and I found my irritation rising. My email communication with this breeder had gone well, but my eyes showed me something else. I felt my empathic senses kick in, telling me this was not a good place.

I paid the $1,000 fee to adopt Lily the kitten, placed her in a crate, and practically ran out of there. Lily was completely quiet on the drive home, and I sensed she was relieved to be gone from that place. I marveled at the fact that Rory, the feral, homeless cat, had become an expensive purebred cat. And what a healthy kitten Lily was! Plump and fluffy, she easily stole our hearts.

Lily is the precocious purring princess of our castle who rules with an iron paw as an adult. She is in charge, and she rules the roost. She demands and orders everyone around. If we don't do things her way, she will meow loudly and scold us. It is quite comical! Lily loudly demands food, demands pets. We can only pet her when she demands it, not when we feel like it. If we fail to pet her when she demands it, she loudly meows in a scolding tone. I understand this is just a part of her personality, but I still wanted to ask her about that behavior.

Lily says, *"You see my behavior as demanding; I see it as assertive. It is all a point of view. There is a difference that you may not realize. Being assertive means asking for what you want or need. I communicate my requests with respect. Being demanding means being inconsiderate to others, their feelings, and their space. I invite you to change your perspective now as I tell you I am assertive. I do not blame you for thinking I am demanding because my behavior might seem like that or might sound like that. When I see you walking towards the kitchen, I run quickly to be petted. I don't want to miss the opportunity. That quick action on my part could be misinterpreted as demanding. In reality, I'm just excited to have a personal moment with you. When you are in the kitchen, and I'm pacing and meowing, I am expressing my excitement for food. I am a foodie like Odie and enjoy meals very much. Sometimes I get so excited I meow in glee. I am not demanding to be fed; I am anticipating the goodness and showing my excitement. Think about all areas of your life where you make assumptions. Please do not assume I'm demanding, as I'm truly just being assertive. You can shift your perspective to see the truth."*

Well, that certainly does change my perspective! It is funny how we human beings have pre-conceived notions about our pet's behavior. I realized I was *assuming* Lily was being demanding, based upon my own human filters. That's one of the reasons I love pet communication so much. It is a tool that helps you understand the truth through your pet's perspective. Now I giggle when Lily is pacing in the kitchen, meowing, knowing she is excited and not being demanding. This makes life more delightful. When you can change your perspective about your pet's behavior, you change your life for the better.

Lily has fallen in love with Odie. Keep in mind that Odie tolerates cats, but he does not like them because they disrupt his peacefulness. Our three cats climb up on countertops and knock things to the floor. If Odie is standing below, he jumps and growls. Lily recognizes that Odie is grumpy and will lay near him, belly up, doing her cutesy paws in the air movement as if saying, "Look at me, Odie, I love you!" Odie will just walk away. His rebuttal never deters Lily's mission to give Odie love. Sometimes she will lick him, and he will snap at her. On rare occasions, they will lay near (but not touching) each other on the couch. I wanted to get Lily's perspective on their relationship.

Lily explains, *"Everyone needs and deserves love. I can sense that Odie holds onto some unneeded fears. When I give him loving attention, I'm asking him to let those go. When you release fear about things that hold you back, you can embrace more love in your heart and feel happier inside. It is my personal purpose to help our family to express more love and feel more love inside. Life is no fun when you are stuck in fear. Love is more fun! I feel Odie is missing out on what life has to offer by always being grumpy and fear-filled. The same holds true for human beings too. When you are willing to look fear in the face, it loses its power over you. Do not be afraid to feel fear. Fear tells you to face it and rise up (face everything and rise). Notice I never stop displaying love to Odie. This is a lesson for everyone that unconditional love never gives up, no matter what."*

Sage words from Lily, who truly understands love. She is helping me to understand cats better. I always thought she was being bossy. In truth, she is leading us out of fear and into love in an assertive way.

She is role modeling that you can still love even when someone frustrates you (like Odie does).

Lily is very independent. Now that I understand she is being assertive and not demanding, I understand her personality better. She exudes self-confidence in her loving assertiveness. Lily knows what she likes and dislikes and lets us know. She is never indecisive. As she sleeps comfortably spread out on the cat tree, so shows us that rest and relaxation are important.

One odd behavior Lily does is darting in front of our feet as we are walking somewhere. This behavior is unsettling because we are afraid of tripping over her. Lily says, *"When I am running in front of your feet, I am not trying to make you trip. I am helping you build greater awareness and slow down. Humans tend to walk through life with blinders on, not noticing the small stuff all around you. That small stuff is beautiful, like the dust particles sparkling in the sunlight. When you can slow down and become more aware around you, you see the magic in life, the beauty of life, the miracles in life. Look down, look up, look around and see what you are missing with those blinders on. Take off your blinders, slow down, and take notice. When you see the beauty of those small things (like me!), you can develop a greater appreciation for life."*

I did ask Lily not to dart in front of our feet, though, as we do not want anyone to get injured. Instead, I asked her to walk next to us and meow loudly, which would cause us to stop to look at her. She agreed that could work, and she's doing that more often now.

Lily has taught me things not easy to learn. She has helped me expand my awareness and not have expectations or assumptions. It took much intentional practice to expand my awareness. I am grateful for all I have learned from Lily. She responds, *"Thank you, Suzanne, for being so open to learning from the Fab Five. I love you!"*

22
LUNA, THE INDEPENDENT INVESTIGATOR

Luna

It was the summer of 2016, and my daughter was working summer school at our local high school. Someone had dumped kittens in the parking lot. A fellow employee scooped up the abandoned kittens and brought them into the office. Well, who doesn't love a cute kitten! My daughter called me to ask if she could bring one home to foster; I said to bring two, so they could play with each other. We planned to foster and then find a good family to adopt them.

Jack and Luna are siblings. Jack is a striped tabby, and Luna is a tuxedo cat. They weighed less than two pounds when we brought them home. Lily did not like nor appreciate that happening. We kept them confined to a bedroom away from everyone else, set on helping them grow and thrive so they could find a new home.

Something happened. You see, my husband has a soft heart for animals. When those two kittens came home, his heart melted. He spent time with them, socializing them and caring for them. The next day we talked about fostering and finding them a home when my husband shouted, "My babies!" That was the end of that discussion, and Jack and Luna became members of the Thibault family.

Luna is a dainty 10 pound, petite cat who is very independent. She would be happiest as the only cat in a family. She is strong-willed and feels she must compete with Jack and Lily. She is an expert at standing up for herself. Many times, Jack is a bully, and she fights back, hissing and swatting at him when he tackles her. Their relationship is contentious.

Luna explains, *"Our arguing behavior is that of most siblings. I love Jack because he's my brother, but I also do not like to be around his bullying, arrogant attitude where he thinks he's the top cat. He tries to boss me around, and I won't have anything to do with it. Our relationship is also speaking volumes that women can stand up for themselves. Never stop standing up for yourself for what you believe is right. Always stand firm against bullying and aggressors. They are weak, and you are the strong one."*

One of Luna's favorite past times is to climb high and knock things down. She truly enjoyed climbing to the top of our nine-foot artificial Christmas tree that crashed to the ground. We no longer put up a Christmas tree. She is the only one of the Fab Five who is fearless. I see her as a strong role model for fearlessness. She is the smallest and the bravest cat, teaching me to be fearless too. The fact that she is fearless and her brother Jack is not, also shows me that fear truly is a state of mind.

Luna says, "Fearlessness can be a choice. You might be scared about many things in life, but it truly is based on your perspective. The path to fearlessness is looking right at fear and seeking the truth because fear is usually connected to a false belief. When you seek the truth, you look at the fear and ask if it is true or not. Usually, you will see fear is all a figment of your imagination. Yes, there are real fears, like with Odie, when something traumatic happens. It is normal to respond in fear, as fear works to keep you safe. I'm talking about those silly mental fears like "I'm not good enough," which keeps you from living the life of your dreams, or "I don't deserve it," or "I can't do that," which holds you back from achieving. When you hear those mental fears in your mind, challenge them and ask yourself if that's true. You will discover that those silly fears are no longer needed in your life. Fearlessness is a choice."

Luna is right! I have had to face many fears and shift them into personal truth. I never considered the inner work I was doing was creating fearlessness, though. I have found inner peace through seeking my truth. Luna's words ring true.

Independent Luna has claimed my husband's lap as her own. Whenever my husband uses the computer, Luna will jump up and interrupt. She will stand right in front of the screen, seeking his lap. He then must pause, tap his lap, and she will lay down there enjoying the cuddling, falling asleep. It is their special bonding time.

Luna says, "I express my love through cuddling. I also enjoy Dad's lap as he is like a radiator of heat, warming me up. Everyone deserves their own quiet space and cuddly connection. This time with Dad is one I cherish. The other animals know this is my space, and they let me be. I appreciate them allowing me private time alone. It is so special and shows you just how smart I am because no one else thought of doing this. The other pets do not even know what they are missing. Cuddling is the best, brightest gift of love around and helps you relax and slow down!"

I often do not even think about slowing down enough to cuddle. Even when we are busy around the house, Luna will show up and ask us to stop and pet her. In this way, she is counseling us to slow down.

I am beginning to see the value of mastering the art of slowing down. That requires mindful awareness of what you are doing instead of running on autopilot. Luna's body language exudes peacefulness. She is a great role model for living a more peace-filled, independent life.

Luna replies, *"The relationship of all of us in our family is beautiful. You are open to seeing our loving guidance and apply it to your own life. This helps you become a better person. I am happy to be a fearless role model of independence."*

23
JACK THE ADVENTURER

Jack

Jack has grown up to be a big boy. He is our largest cat with the most energy. His start outdoors fueled his adventurous spirit. Becoming an indoor cat, he does spaz runs throughout the house, parlaying off the glass slider door. He can jump high and wide, enjoying the adventure of movement. He also enjoys exploring every nook and cranny of every closet, drawer, bag, and box. Once we noticed this active behavior, we decided to purchase a cat wheel for him to run on. He enjoys walking on it each night.

Jack says, *"Life is an adventure! My life started in the wilds. I was rescued and found my way into your family. For that, I am grateful! Adventure can be had at any given moment. Life is not about sitting on the sidelines watching. It is about seeking adventure, having fun, living fully. I am modeling this for you through my adventurous behavior. You all tend to sit around when you are unsure what you want to do. I say make some plans! Seek adventures! Live life to the fullest! Do not let life pass you by when you have it within your power to seek and go after what you want. Seek and find the adventure in life."*

So much wisdom! Jack is teaching many things through his adventurous behavior. He is showing us his personality and how much he enjoys life. Jack is an excellent hunter. Total pandemonium ensues with our three cats when a fly enters the house. The hunt is on! They leap, run, and jump after the fly, which is completely outnumbered. I can always tell when Jack is about to pounce, as he squats down, gives a little butt wiggle, then bam, swats at the fly, knocking it to the ground.

Jack replies, *"You should always hunt down what you want out of life. Sometimes things might land in your lap, but most of the time, you must go hunting. My butt wiggle is showing you I am hyper-focused upon what I want. You can do this too. You need to focus on what you want and hunt it, but butt wiggling is optional. It might seem elusive, but if you have determination, you will be successful. What I am describing to you is the spiritual walk of life. It is up to you to decide what you want, seek it out, and develop the determination to succeed."*

Who knew adventurous cats could also impart wisdom! I believe Jack is also a counselor. One day, Jack was trapped inside my home office. I heard meowing coming from my office. I opened the door, and there was Jack. He was trapped in the office all night; I wasn't even aware he was in there. He came running out. As I looked around, I saw the destruction. He has clawed at the door frame repeatedly, damaging the weather stripping. He had also knocked things over onto the floor.

I apologized to him, and he easily forgave our mistake of not counting cats before bed. He drank a lot of water, peed, and relaxed in his normal resting spot. Jack says, "*I wanted to share something for your own personal growth. I believe you feel trapped in your day job and are scratching to get out and do what you love, your true purpose.*"

Ouch! Jack was right! At that time, I was working a full-time day job and pursuing my small business, working 60 hours per week. It was like Jack peered inside my heart and soul, saw my inner struggles, and showed me through his behavior. What an amazing counselor Jack is! I am truly blessed to live with five fabulous pets who care so much about my personal and spiritual wellbeing.

The Fab Five have truly helped me open my heart and heal my soul wounds. They have shown me aspects about myself that I never realized were keeping me stuck. Lacking self-confidence, impatience, intolerance, and making assumptions limited me. The Fab Five are a complete package of loving guidance I embrace and hug each day. Their love knows no bounds!

I am eternally grateful for these five furry, loving relationships that have taught me so much. My life has improved immensely in learning from them. I hope you will allow your pet to guide you in life; understanding their guidance is also God's guidance. Proper life guidance comes in many forms. The best counselor has fur and four paws.

24
PLUS ONE: WATSON THE REBEL HAMSTER

Watson

As a teen, my daughter was working at a locally owned pet store. This is where she met a brave hamster she named Watson, after Sherlock Holmes and Watson. The hamster had been in a group pen with one other hamster. A fight ensued, and Watson was injured, with a cut in his ear and nose. She took Watson into the back room to separate him from the other hamster and tend to his wounds. She called the store owner to ask if she could take Watson home to care for him, and home he came, becoming our plus one.

We purchased hamster supplies for Watson. He was traumatized by the fight and wound and hid in a tube in his cage. It was fun having a hamster in our home with three adults. At this point, we had no cats, so all was well.

Watson said, *"We got in a fight over food. The other hamster was being mean, trying to hoard all the food, not allowing me to eat. I rebelled, stood up to the bully, and won freedom in the process. Sure, I got injured, but your loving care helped me heal and find a home in the process!"*

It took Watson a few weeks to heal. We noticed he was feeling better when he began running on his wheel. He enjoyed all sorts of food and goodies he would stuff in his cheeks. Watson modeled pure delight in living life. He was curious with a rebel spirit. He would stand on his back legs a lot to look around, standing his ground.

Watson explains, *"My rebel spirit speaks volumes to you, so listen up! I am a rebel with a cause. Not a cause to hurt, but to stand up for yourself. A rebel mindset means you can do things differently, not go along with the norm of social ideas. You can think outside the box, make healthy choices, and be your own advocate for the life you want. That's what being a rebel means to me. May it inspire you!"*

After about eight months, we were talking about adopting our first cat. We knew Watson would not enjoy a cat, so we decided to put Watson up for adoption. A schoolteacher and her young daughter adopted Watson. He was so happy! He touched our hearts with his rebel spirit!

25
CONCLUDING THOUGHTS

I hope your heart has been touched by these wonderful stories, as much as we have enjoyed sharing them with you. My wish for you is that the truth of these relationships, the insightful lessons learned, and the inspiring messages these guest authors and their pets have shared may empower you in your relationship with animals. We can all be animal advocates and support our furry, feathered, scaley friends by embracing unconditional love and sharing it outward with everyone.

If you enjoyed this book, I invite you to read *Animal Wisdom Tales: Messages of Love from Pets and Wild Animals*, available on Amazon. For that book, I interviewed more than 80 animals, asking them one question, "What wisdom would you like to share with human beings to help us better understand life?" Their responses provide profound guidance that can transform how you view the world around you from the animal's perspective.

Are you interested in connecting with other animal lovers? Join me in the Pet Communication and Healing Facebook Community for inspiration and connection. Want to learn the foundations of pet communication? Visit Suzanne Thibault Academy and enroll for free in the Pet Communication 101 online course. Have a misbehaving pet? You can download a free E-book, *My Pet Did What?! Understanding Stress, Anxiety and PTSD with Your Empathic Pet.*

26
BONUS AND RESOURCES

Book Bonus:
Free Chapter: Pets and Toxins
Receive a free chapter from award winning author Cheryl Meyer's book, *Feeling Good: Living Low Toxin in Community and Everyday Life*. You can receive the chapter Introduction to Pets - Pets and Toxins (https://bit.ly/toxincandpets) which has valueable information on toxins that can affect pet health.

To learn more about the authors:

Suzanne Thibault - https://www.suzannethibault.net

Cathe - https://www.facebook.com/LookWhatBeautyGodMade

Cheryl Meyer - https://cherylmhealthmuse.com/ and https://heavenlytreepress.com/

Darcie Litwicki - https://www.silverheartranch.com/

Karen Takayama – https://shinedirectory.org

Suzanne Ellison - https://suzanneellison.coach/

Tanya Lochner - https://tanyalochner.com/

ABOUT THE AUTHOR

Suzanne is a pet empath, communicator, and spiritual life coach serving animal lovers to effectively communicate with animals for a healthy relationship. She seeks to end emotional suffering for both people and animals as she has overcome her childhood trauma. Grateful for her spiritual gifts, she supports through pet conversations to bring healing to the heart and divine inner healing with Holy Spirit. Her pets have helped to guide the way and teach her how to support animals spiritually while growing on a personal level.

Her core message, *Love Makes All Things Possible*, was born from her childhood dog Wiggles, saving her life as a child growing up in a highly toxic family. Through her podcast, Spiritual Straight Talk, Suzanne inspires awareness of spiritual self-care and animal emotional wellbeing and relationships. As the founder of Suzanne Thibault Academy, she provides pet communication training programs.

Suzanne is a volunteer for Red Rover Responder, a non-profit organization providing emergency safety for animals through shelter and care during natural disasters and crises. She and her husband are also American Red Cross Disaster Assistance Team members. Her altruistic work is her way of giving back to people and animals to help end suffering, in gratitude for all the gifts and blessings she has received from Spirit and animals.

www.ingramcontent.com/pod-product-compliance
Lightning Source LLC
Chambersburg PA
CBHW071900070526
44583CB00016B/1775